NETSCAPE
NAVIGATOR

AN INTRODUCTION

Gary B. Shelly
Thomas J. Cashman
Kurt A. Jordan

An International Thomson Publishing Company

Danvers • Albany • Bonn • Boston • Cincinnati • Detroit • London • Madrid • Melbourne
Mexico City • New York • Paris • San Francisco • Singapore • Tokyo • Toronto • Washington

boyd & fraser
publishing company

SHELLY
CASHMAN
SERIES®

© 1996 boyd & fraser publishing company
One Corporate Place • Ferncroft Village
Danvers, Massachusetts 01923

I(T)P   International Thomson Publishing
boyd & fraser publishing company is an ITP company
The ITP trademark is used under license.

Printed in the United States of America

For more information, contact boyd & fraser publishing company:

boyd & fraser publishing company
One Corporate Place • Ferncroft Village
Danvers, Massachusetts 01923, USA

International Thomson Publishing Europe
Berkshire House
168-173 High Holborn
London, WC1V 7AA, United Kingdom

Thomas Nelson Australia
102 Dodds Street
South Melbourne
Victoria 3205 Australia

Nelson Canada
1120 Birchmont Road
Scarborough, Ontario
Canada M1K 5G4

International Thomson Editores
Campos Eliseos 385, Piso 7
Colonia Polanco
11560 Mexico D.F. Mexico

International Thomson Publishing GmbH
Konigswinterer Strasse 418
53227 Bonn, Germany

International Thomson Publishing Asia
Block 211, Henderson Road #08-03
Henderson Industrial Park
Singapore 0315

International Thomson Publishing Japan
Hirakawa-cho Kyowa Building, 3F
2-2-1 Hirakawa-cho, Chiyoda-ku
Tokyo 102, Japan

ISBN 0-7895-0320-4

2 3 4 5 6 7 8 9 10   BC   0 9 8 7 6

This book was designed using Quark 3.31 for Windows and CorelDraw 5.0 for Windows.

CONTENTS

NETSCAPE NAVIGATOR
An Introduction · N1

WELCOME TO NETSCAPE

ESCAPES · COMPANY & PRODUCTS · NETSCAPE STORE · NEWS & REFERENCE · ASSISTANCE · COMMUNITY

PREFACE

▶ SHELLY CASHMAN SERIES

The Shelly Cashman Series offers superior materials from which to learn about computers. In addition to computer concepts, programming, networking, and the Internet, the Shelly Cashman Series is proud to present both Windows- and DOS-based personal computer applications in a variety of traditionally bound textbooks. The table on page vii shows the available books in the Shelly Cashman Series.

If you do not find the exact Shelly Cashman Series book to fit your needs, boyd & fraser's unique **Custom Edition** program allows you to choose from a number of options and create a textbook perfectly suited to your course. This exciting program is explained and summarized in the table on page viii.

▶ THE WORLD WIDE WEB

Since its birth in 1989, the World Wide Web, or Web for short, has grown at a rapid pace. Within only a few years, the Web has increased from a limited number of networked computers to thousands of computers located all over the world available to millions of users. Schools, businesses, and the computing industry all are taking advantage of this new way of accessing the Internet to provide products, services, and education electronically. Netscape Navigator provides the novice as well as the experienced user a window with which to look into the Web and tap an abundance of resources all available at the click of a mouse button. The World Wide Web is within reach of anyone with a computer, modem, and the proper software. Thus, an up-to-date educational institution that teaches students how to use computers much teach Web basics.

Educational and charitable nonprofit institutions can obtain, free of charge, Netscape Navigator and Netscape Communications Server from Netscape Communications Corporation. The Netscape Navigator is the browser presented in this textbook. The Communications Server enables organizations to publish hypermedia documents on the World Wide Web. For more information, call (415) 528-2555.

▶ OBJECTIVES OF THIS TEXTBOOK

Netscape Navigator: An Introduction is intended for use in combination with a variety of computer instruction. Specific objectives of this book are as follows:

▸ To teach the fundamentals of how the World Wide Web works
▸ To teach the student how to use Netscape Navigator to access the World Wide Web
▸ To expose the student to the various available World Wide Web services
▸ To develop an exercise-oriented approach that allows the student to learn by example
▸ To help the student understand what can be accomplished using Netscape Navigator
▸ To encourage curiosity and independent exploration of World Wide Web resources
▸ To serve as a primer on how to use the World Wide Web

▶ ORGANIZATION OF THIS TEXTBOOK

*N*etscape Navigator: An Introduction consists of two projects that cover accessing the World Wide Web using Netscape and two appendices. Appendix A lists popular World Wide Web sites categorized by topic. Appendix B contains instructions for installing an electronic mail program called Eudora that is used in the electronic mail section of Project 2.

Each project begins with a statement of objectives. A project summary and list of key terms are provided at the end of each project. The key terms are highlighted in bold when first introduced in the project. Questions and exercises are presented at the end of each project. Exercises include short answer and hands-on assignments. The projects and appendices are organized as follows:

Project 1 – Introduction to Netscape   In Project 1, students are introduced to the World Wide Web and its components. Topics include how the Web is organized, browsing Web pages, Web page management techniques, saving and printing material obtained from a Web site, and communicating with other people on the Web.

Project 2 – Searching, Retrieving, and Conversing Using Netscape   In Project 2, students begin to explore the potential of the World Wide Web. Topics include techniques for searching the vast amount of materials available on the Web using search engines such as InfoSeek and WebCrawler, using traditional Internet services such as FTP and gopher through Netscape, and conversing with other people using news groups and electronic mail.

Appendix A – Popular Web Sites   Appendix A lists the URLs of popular Web sites by topics. Topics include art, business, entertainment, government, Internet relay chat, jobs, law, miscellaneous, museums, music, shopping, and FTP and gopher sites.

Appendix B – Installing the Eudora Mail Program   Appendix B contains instructions for installing the Eudora electronic mail program for Windows. A popular shareware mail program, Eudora is available at numerous FTP sites on the Internet. Eudora is used in the section on electronic mail in Project 2.

▶ ANCILLARY MATERIALS FOR TEACHING FROM THIS SHELLY CASHMAN SERIES TEXTBOOK

comprehensive instructor's support package accompanies all textbooks in the Shelly Cashman Series.

Instructor's Manual   The Instructor's Manual contains the following:
- ▶ Detailed lesson plans including project objectives, project overview, and lecture notes with page references and illustration references
- ▶ Answers to all the student exercises at the end of the projects
- ▶ A test bank of True/False, Multiple Choice, and Fill-in questions
- ▶ Selected master transparencies

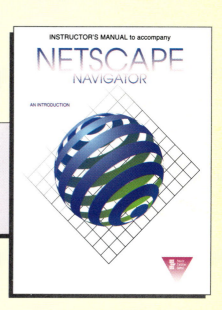

ElecMan   ElecMan stands for *Electronic Man*ual. ElecMan is the Instructor's Manual on diskette. This diskette allows an instructor to use any Windows word processor to modify the lecture notes or generate quizzes and exams from the test bank.

Figures on CD-ROM   Illustrations for every screen in the textbook are on a CD-ROM. Using this CD-ROM, an instructor can create a slide show or print and make transparencies for a lecture presentation.

MicroExam IV   MicroExam IV, a computerized test-generating system, is available free to adopters of any Shelly Cashman Series textbooks. It includes all of the questions from the test bank just described. MicroExam IV is an easy-to-use, menu-driven software package that provides instructors with testing flexibility and allows customizing of testing documents.

NetTest IV   NetTest IV allows instructors to take a MicroExam IV file made up of True/False and Multiple Choice questions and proctor a paperless examination in a network environment. The same questions display in a different order on each PC. Students have the option of instantaneous feedback. Tests are electronically graded, and an item analysis is produced.

▶ ACKNOWLEDGMENTS

The Shelly Cashman Series would not be the success it is without the contributions of outstanding publishing professionals. First, and foremost, among them is Becky Herrington, director of production and designer. She is the heart and soul of the Shelly Cashman Series and it is only through her leadership, dedication, and untiring efforts that superior products are produced.

Under Becky's direction, the following individuals made significant contributions to this book: Ginny Harvey, series administrator and manuscript editor; Peter Schiller, production manager; Ken Russo, senior illustrator; Mike Bodnar, Greg Herrington, and Dave Bonnewitz, illustrators; Jeanne Black and Betty Hopkins, typographers; Tracy Murphy, series coordinator; Marilyn Martin and Nancy Lamm, proofreaders; Cristina Haley, indexer; Dennis Tani, cover design; and Patti Garbarino, office manager.

Special recognition for a job well done must go to Jim Quasney, who, together with writing, assumed the responsibilities as series editor. Particular thanks go to Thomas Walker, president and CEO of boyd & fraser publishing company.

We hope you will find using this book an enriching and rewarding experience.

Gary B. Shelly
Thomas J. Cashman
Kurt A. Jordan

▶ SHELLY CASHMAN SERIES – TRADITIONALLY BOUND TEXTBOOKS

The Shelly Cashman Series presents both Windows- and DOS-based personal computer applications in a variety of traditionally bound textbooks, as shown in the table below. For more information, see your ITP representative or call 1-800-423-0563.

COMPUTERS	
Computers	Using Computers: A Gateway to Information
	Using Computers: A Gateway to Information, Brief Edition
	Study Guide for Using Computers: A Gateway to Information
Computers and Windows Applications	Using Computers: A Gateway to Information and Microsoft Office (also available in spiral bound)
	Using Computers: A Gateway to Information and Microsoft Works 3.0 (also available in spiral bound)
	Complete Computer Concepts and Microsoft Works 2.0 (also available in spiral bound)
Computers and DOS Applications	Complete Computer Concepts and WordPerfect 5.1, Lotus 1-2-3 Release 2.2, and dBASE IV Version 1.1 (also available in spiral bound)
	Complete Computer Concepts and WordPerfect 5.1, Lotus 1-2-3 Release 2.2, and dBASE III PLUS
Computers and Programming	Using Computers: A Gateway to Information and Programming in QBasic

WINDOWS APPLICATIONS	
Integrated Packages	Microsoft Office: Introductory Concepts and Techniques (also available in spiral bound)
	Microsoft Office: Advanced Concepts and Techniques (also available in spiral bound)
	Microsoft Works 3.0 (also available in spiral bound)*
	Microsoft Works 3.0—Short Course
	Microsoft Works 2.0 (also available in spiral bound)
Windows	Microsoft Windows 3.1 Introductory Concepts and Techniques
	Microsoft Windows 3.1 Complete Concepts and Techniques
Windows Applications	Microsoft Word 2.0, Microsoft Excel 4, and Paradox 1.0 (also available in spiral bound)
Word Processing	Microsoft Word 6* • Microsoft Word 2.0
	WordPerfect 6.1* • WordPerfect 6* • WordPerfect 5.2
Spreadsheets	Microsoft Excel 5* • Microsoft Excel 4
	Lotus 1-2-3 Release 5* • Lotus 1-2-3 Release 4*
	Quattro Pro 6 • Quattro Pro 5
Database Management	Paradox 5 • Paradox 4.5 • Paradox 1.0
	Microsoft Access 2*
	Visual dBASE 5/5.5
Presentation Graphics	Microsoft PowerPoint 4*

DOS APPLICATIONS	
Operating Systems	DOS 6 Introductory Concepts and Techniques
	DOS 6 and Microsoft Windows 3.1 Introductory Concepts and Techniques
Integrated Package	Microsoft Works 3.0 (also available in spiral bound)
DOS Applications	WordPerfect 5.1, Lotus 1-2-3 Release 2.2, and dBASE IV Version 1.1 (also available in spiral bound)
	WordPerfect 5.1, Lotus 1-2-3 Release 2.2, and dBASE III PLUS (also available in spiral bound)
Word Processing	WordPerfect 6.0
	WordPerfect 5.1 Step-by-Step Function Key Edition
	WordPerfect 5.1
	WordPerfect 5.1 Function Key Edition
	WordPerfect 4.2 (with Educational Software)
	WordStar 6.0 (with Educational Software)
Spreadsheets	Lotus 1-2-3 Release 4 • Lotus 1-2-3 Release 2.4 • Lotus 1-2-3 Release 2.3
	Lotus 1-2-3 Release 2.2 • Lotus 1-2-3 Release 2.01
	Quattro Pro 3.0
	Quattro with 1-2-3 Menus (with Educational Software)
Database Management	dBASE 5
	dBASE IV Version 1.1
	dBASE III PLUS (with Educational Software)
	Paradox 4.5
	Paradox 3.5 (with Educational Software)

PROGRAMMING AND NETWORKING	
Programming	Microsoft Visual Basic 3.0 for Windows*
	Microsoft BASIC
	QBasic
Networking	Novell NetWare for Users
Internet	The Internet: Introductory Concepts and Techniques (UNIX)
	Netscape Navigator: An Introduction

*Also available as a Double Diamond Edition, which is a shortened version of the complete book

▶ SHELLY CASHMAN SERIES – Custom Edition PROGRAM

If you do not find a Shelly Cashman Series traditionally bound textbook to fit your needs, boyd & fraser's unique **Custom Edition** program allows you to choose from a number of options and create a textbook perfectly suited to your course. The customized materials are available in a variety of binding styles, including boyd & fraser's patented **Custom Edition** kit, spiral bound, and notebook bound. Features of the **Custom Edition** program are:

- ▶ Textbooks that match the content of your course
- ▶ Windows- and DOS-based materials for the latest versions of personal computer applications software
- ▶ Shelly Cashman Series quality, with the same full-color materials and Shelly Cashman Series pedagogy found in the traditionally bound books
- ▶ Affordable pricing so your students receive the **Custom Edition** at a cost similar to that of traditionally bound books

The table on the right summarizes the available materials. For more information, see your ITP representative or call 1-800-423-0563.

COMPUTERS	
Computers	Using Computers: A Gateway to Information
	Using Computers: A Gateway to Information, Brief Edition
	Study Guide for Using Computers: A Gateway to Information
	Introduction to Computers (32-page)
OPERATING SYSTEMS	
Windows	Microsoft Windows 3.1 Introductory Concepts and Techniques
	Microsoft Windows 3.1 Complete Concepts and Techniques
DOS	Introduction to DOS 6 (using DOS prompt)
	Introduction to DOS 5.0 (using DOS shell)
	Introduction to DOS 5.0 or earlier (using DOS prompt)
WINDOWS APPLICATIONS	
Integrated Packages	Microsoft Works 3.0*
	Microsoft Works 3.0—Short Course
	Microsoft Works 2.0
Microsoft Office	Using Microsoft Office (16-page)
	Object Linking and Embedding (OLE) (32-page)
Word Processing	Microsoft Word 6*
	Microsoft Word 2.0
	WordPerfect 6.1*
	WordPerfect 6*
	WordPerfect 5.2
Spreadsheets	Microsoft Excel 5*
	Microsoft Excel 4
	Lotus 1-2-3 Release 5*
	Lotus 1-2-3 Release 4*
	Quattro Pro 6
	Quattro Pro 5
Database Management	Paradox 5
	Paradox 4.5
	Paradox 1.0
	Microsoft Access 2*
	Visual dBASE 5/5.5
Presentation Graphics	Microsoft PowerPoint 4*
DOS APPLICATIONS	
Integrated Package	Microsoft Works 3.0
Word Processing	WordPerfect 6.0
	WordPerfect 5.1 Step-by-Step Function Key Edition
	WordPerfect 5.1
	WordPerfect 5.1 Function Key Edition
	Microsoft Word 5.0
	WordPerfect 4.2
	WordStar 6.0
Spreadsheets	Lotus 1-2-3 Release 4
	Lotus 1-2-3 Release 2.4
	Lotus 1-2-3 Release 2.3
	Lotus 1-2-3 Release 2.2
	Lotus 1-2-3 Release 2.01
	Quattro Pro 3.0
	Quattro with 1-2-3 Menus
Database Management	dBASE 5
	dBASE IV Version 1.1
	dBASE III PLUS
	Paradox 4.5
	Paradox 3.5
PROGRAMMING AND NETWORKING	
Programming	Microsoft Visual Basic 3.0 for Windows*
	Microsoft BASIC
	QBasic
Networking	Novell NetWare for Users
Internet	The Internet: Introductory Concepts and Techniques (UNIX)
	Netscape Navigator: An Introduction

* Also available as a mini-module

NETSCAPE
NAVIGATOR

AN INTRODUCTION

NETSCAPE
NAVIGATOR

INTRODUCTION TO NETSCAPE

OBJECTIVES You will have mastered the material in this project when you can:

▸ Define the Internet
▸ Describe hypermedia and browsers
▸ Explain a hypermedia link
▸ Start Netscape
▸ Describe Netscape features
▸ Maneuver through the history list
▸ Create and remove bookmarks
▸ Save Web pages on a diskette

▸ Print Web pages
▸ Save graphic images on a diskette
▸ Print graphic images
▸ Copy and paste from Web pages using the Clipboard
▸ Send information over the Internet using forms
▸ Use Netscape's Help features

▸ INTRODUCTION

One of the more popular and fastest growing areas in computing today is the Internet. Using the Internet, you can do research, get stock quotes, shop for services and merchandise, display weather maps, obtain pictures, movies, audio clips, and information stored on computers around the world, and converse with people worldwide.

Once considered mysterious, the Internet is now accessible to the general public because personal computers with user-friendly tools have reduced its complexity. The Internet, with hundreds of thousands of connected computers, continues to grow with thousands of new users coming online every month. Now, businesses, newspapers, television stations, even the White House, are on the Internet; but, just exactly what is the Internet?

▸ DEFINITION OF THE INTERNET

The **Internet** is a collection of networks (Figure 1-1), each of which is composed of a collection of smaller networks; for example, on a college campus, the network in the student lab can be connected to the faculty computer network, which is connected to the administration network, and they all can connect to the Internet.

Networks are connected with high-, medium- and low-speed data lines that allow data to move from one computer to another. The separate networks connect to the Internet through computers.

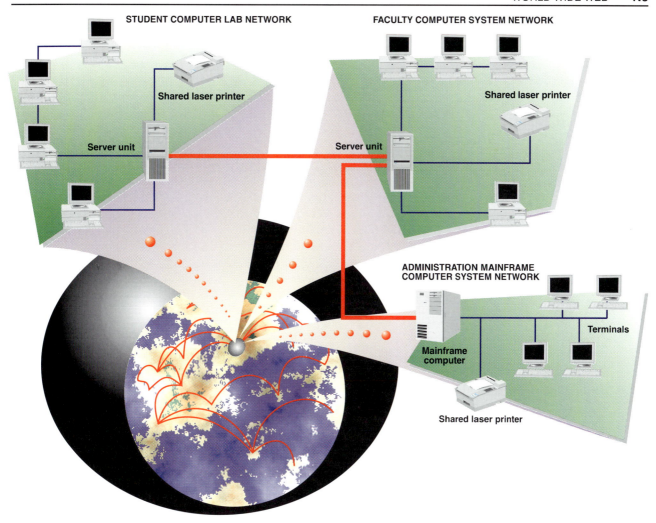

FIGURE 1-1

▶ WORLD WIDE WEB

Modern computer systems have the capability to deliver information in a variety of ways, such as graphics, sound, video clips, animation, and, of course, regular text. On the Internet, this multimedia capability is available in a form called **hypermedia**, which is any variety of computer media, including text, graphics, video, and sound.

Hypermedia is accessed through the use of a **hypertext link**, or simply **link**, which is a special software pointer that points to the location of the computer on which the hypermedia is stored and to the hypermedia itself. A link can point to hypermedia on any computer hooked into the Internet that is running the proper software. Thus, a hypertext link on a computer in New York can point to a picture on a computer in Los Angeles.

To cause a picture stored on a computer in Los Angeles to display on a computer in New York, the user in New York need merely click an object such as text or a drawing that, through the use of special instructions, has been designated as a link to the picture in Los Angeles. The picture will display automatically in New York.

The collection of hypertext links throughout the Internet creates an interconnected network of links called the **World Wide Web**, which is also referred to as the **Web**, or **WWW**.

Each computer within the Web containing hypermedia that can be referenced by hypertext links is called a **Web site**. Thousands of Web sites around the world can be accessed through the Internet.

Pictures or other hypermedia available at Web sites are stored in files called **documents**, or **Web pages**. Therefore, when you click a hypertext linked object to display a picture, read text, view a video, or listen to a song, you are actually viewing a Web page or part of a Web page that contains the hypermedia. Each Web page has a unique address that identifies it from all other pages on the Internet.

Home Pages

No main menus or any particular starting points exist in the World Wide Web. Although you can reference any page in the Internet when you begin, most people start with specially designated pages called home pages. A **home page** is the first page for a Web site. All other Web pages at that site can usually be reached through a site's home page. In addition, the home page is the default page that displays on your computer if you do not know the address of any other pages located at a particular Web site.

Because it is the starting point for most Web sites, the sites try to make a good first impression and create an attractive home page, with eye-catching graphics, specially formatted text, and a variety of hypertext links to hypermedia contained both at the Web site and at other interesting and useful Web sites.

Internet Browsers

Just as graphical user interfaces (GUIs) such as Microsoft Windows make using a computer easier, **browsers** such as Netscape Navigator (Netscape for short) make using the World Wide Web easier by removing the complexity of having to remember the syntax of commands to reference Web pages at Web sites.

Mosaic, the first Internet browser, ignited the rise in popularity of the World Wide Web. Netscape, from Netscape Communications Corporation, was developed by some of the same people who wrote Mosaic, keeping the best parts of Mosaic and adding new, user-friendly features.

▶ STARTING NETSCAPE

T o start Netscape, the Windows Program Manager must display on the screen and the Netscape group window must be open. Perform the following steps to start Netscape.

TO START NETSCAPE ▼

STEP 1 ▶

Use the mouse to point to the Netscape program-item icon in the Netscape group window (Figure 1-2).

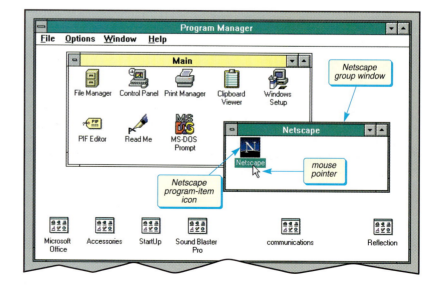

FIGURE 1-2

STEP 2 ▶

Double-click the left mouse button.

The Welcome To Netscape home page displays, indicating you have connected to Netscape Communications Corporation's computer Web site (Figure 1-3). The appearance of this page may display differently on your computer. Netscape Communications Corporation changes its home page often by adding announcements and other interesting elements that provide continuous updates and information.

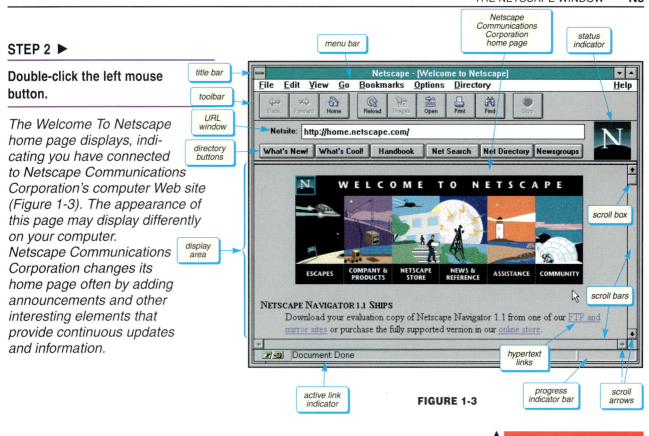

FIGURE 1-3

When Netscape starts, your computer is connected to a computer at Netscape Communications Corporation. The Welcome To Netscape home page displays in the **title bar** at the top of the screen.

▶ THE NETSCAPE WINDOW

T he Netscape window (Figure 1-3) consists of features to make browsing the Internet easy. It contains a title bar, menu bar, toolbar, URL window, status indicator, directory buttons, scroll bars, scroll box, and scroll arrows, a progress indicator, and a display area where pages from the World Wide Web display.

With most pages, only a portion of the page is visible on your screen. You view the portion of the page displayed on the screen through the **display area**. To the right and at the bottom of the display area are scroll bars, scroll arrows, and a scroll box, which you can use to move the display area up and down or left and right to reveal other parts of the page.

The menu bar, toolbar, URL window, status indicator, and directory buttons appear at the top of the screen just below the title bar. The progress indicator appears at the bottom of the screen.

Notice in Figure 1-3 the underlined blue words toward the bottom of the Netscape home page. The blue color and underlining identify those phrases as hypertext links. Clicking retrieves the linked Web page and displays it on your screen. When placed over a hypertext link, the mouse pointer changes to a pointing hand.

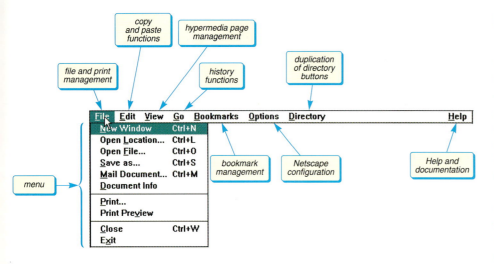

FIGURE 1-4

Menu Bar

The **menu bar** displays Netscape menu names (Figure 1-4). Each menu name represents a menu of commands that you can use to perform actions such as saving Web pages on a diskette, sending mail, managing bookmarks, setting Netscape options, and accessing frequently used Internet services. To display a menu, such as the File menu in Figure 1-4, select it by pointing to the menu name File and clicking the left mouse button. To perform an action, choose the command on the menu by pointing to the command name and clicking the left mouse button.

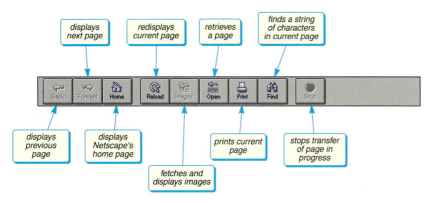

FIGURE 1-5

Toolbar and Directory Buttons

The **toolbar** and **directory buttons** contain buttons that allow you to perform frequent tasks more quickly than when using the menu bar. For example, to print the page being displayed, click the Print button on the toolbar.

Each button on the toolbar contains a word and an icon describing its function. Figures 1-5 and 1-6 illustrate the toolbar and directory buttons and briefly describe the functions of the buttons. Each of the buttons will be explained in detail as they are used.

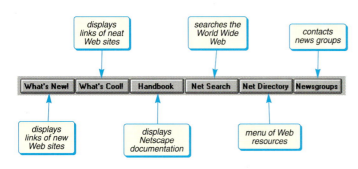

FIGURE 1-6

URL Window

Each Web page is identified by a special address called the Universal Resource Locator. A **Universal Resource Locator** or **URL** (pronounced *you are ell*) is important because it is the unique address of each Web page at the Web sites on the World Wide Web.

A typical URL is composed of three parts (Figure 1-7). The first is the protocol. A **protocol** is a set of rules computers follow. Most Web pages use HTTP. **HTTP** stands for HyperText Transport Protocol. HTTP describes the rules for transmitting hypermedia documents electronically. The protocol is entered in lowercase as http, and is followed by a colon and two slashes.

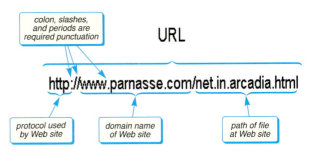

FIGURE 1-7

The second part is the domain name. The **domain name** is the Internet address of the computer on the Internet where the Web page is located. The domain name includes periods and is followed by one slash.

The third part is the file specification of the Web page. The file specification includes the filename and possibly a directory or folder name. This information is called the **path**.

URLs that point to interesting Web pages can be found in magazines, newspapers, browsing the Web, or from friends. Because of the variety and numbers of URLs, you may find it useful to keep a directory of URLs. Netscape has facilities for saving and organizing your favorite URLs so you can access them easily. Later in this project, you will save and recall URLs.

The **URL window** (Figure 1-8) contains the Universal Resource Locator for the page currently shown in the display area of Netscape. It will be updated automatically as you browse from page to page over the World Wide Web. You can also indicate a Web site to connect to by dragging the mouse pointer over the current URL in the window, typing in a valid URL, and pressing the ENTER key.

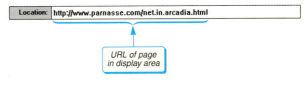

FIGURE 1-8

Status Indicator and Progress Indicator

The **status indicator** (Figure 1-9), which is also Netscape Communications Corporation's company logo, goes into motion, or animates, while a connection to a Web site is being made and while a page is being retrieved and displayed. At the bottom right of the Netscape window, is a **progress indicator** (Figure 1-10). Acting much like a thermometer, it indicates how much of the accessed page has been received from the Web site.

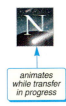

FIGURE 1-9

Active Link Indicator

If the mouse pointer is positioned over an object that has been linked to a Web page, the **active link indicator** displays the URL that will be used to retrieve the page. In addition, if a Web page is being received, the active link indicator provides information about the progress of the transfer of the page (Figure 1-10).

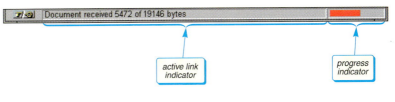

FIGURE 1-10

▶ BROWSING THE WORLD WIDE WEB

T he Welcome To Netscape page provides a starting point for browsing the World Wide Web. Some of the more interesting and newer pages can be reached by taking advantage of the directory buttons What's New (What's New!) and What's Cool (What's Cool!). If you click the What's New button, Netscape displays the What's New page with links to the some of the newer Web pages. If you click the What's Cool button, Netscape displays the What's Cool page with links to the some of the neatest Web pages.

Netscape Communications Corporation updates the What's New and What's Cool pages often as new and extraordinary Web pages become available, so links that appear one day may be gone the next, replaced with new offerings.

Two other buttons on the Welcome To Netscape page that allow you to browse the World Wide Web are the directory buttons Net Search (Net Search) and Net Directory (Net Directory). These two buttons allow you to search for topics in which you may be interested. Both buttons will be discussed in detail in Project 2.

The most common way to browse the World Wide Web is to obtain the URL of a Web page you want to visit and enter it into the URL window. Appendix A lists the URLs of some of the more frequently visited Web pages. Practice using Netscape by visiting some of those listed. It is by visiting various Web sites that you can begin to understand the enormous appeal of the World Wide Web. The following steps show you how to visit the Web page titled Net in Arcadia, which contains the art works and information about various classicist artists. The URL for the Net in Arcadia page is http://www.parnasse.com/net.in. arcadia.html.

TO BROWSE THE WORLD WIDE WEB BY ENTERING A URL ▼

STEP 1 ▶

Point to the beginning of the URL window and drag across the current URL.

The current URL is highlighted in the URL window (Figure 1-11).

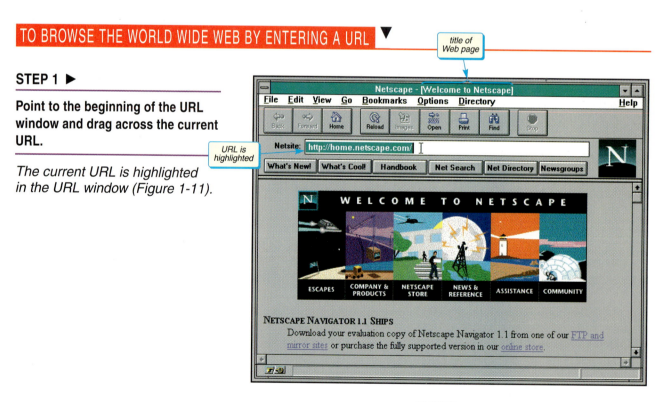

FIGURE 1-11

STEP 2 ▶

Type http://www.parnasse.com/net.in.arcadia.html

The new URL displays in the URL window (Figure 1-12). If you type the wrong letter or symbol in the URL window and notice the error before you move on to the next step, use the BACKSPACE *key to erase all the characters back to and including the one that is wrong and then continue typing.*

FIGURE 1-12

STEP 3 ▶

Press the ENTER **key.**

Netscape begins the transfer of the Net in Arcadia page from the Web site to your computer. The gray icon in the Stop button on the toolbar changes to red. A message appears in the active link indicator at the bottom of the screen and the progress indicator moves to the right, both providing information about the progress of the transfer. The page starts to display in the display area (Figure 1-13) When the transfer is complete, a message appears in the active link indicator indicating the transfer is complete. The Stop sign icon returns to gray and the status indicator motion stops.

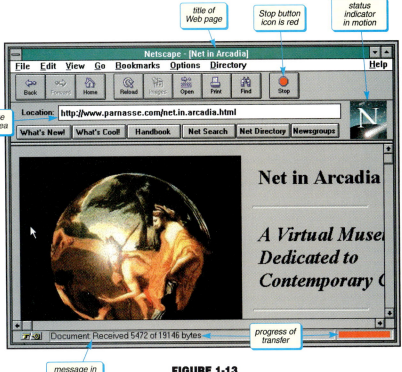

FIGURE 1-13

STEP 4 ▶

Using the scroll box on the vertical scroll bar on the right side of the window, scroll the window down until the blue Works by Andree Descharnes link displays. Position the mouse pointer anywhere in the picture.

The shape of the mouse pointer changes to a pointing hand (Figure 1-14). This change indicates the picture, as well as the words next to it, have been set up as a hypermedia link.

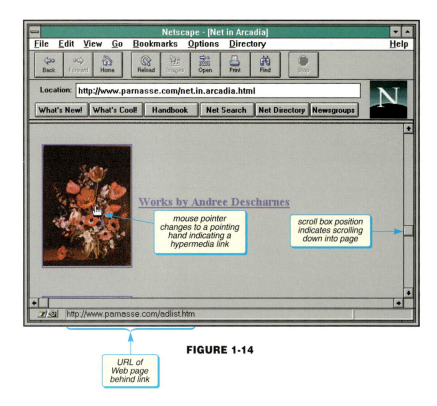

FIGURE 1-14

STEP 5 ▶

Click the picture.

The page starts to display in the display area (Figure 1-15). The Andree Descharnes page is larger than the display area, so you will have to scroll down to reveal the paintings that are available for display.

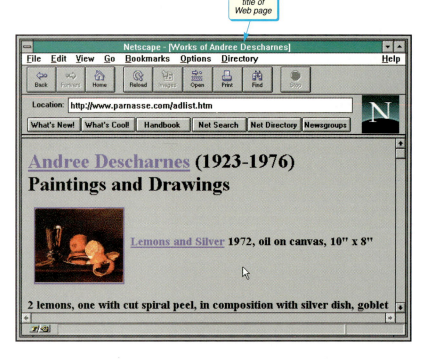

FIGURE 1-15

STEP 6 ▶

Scroll down until the Flowers in a Vase link displays. Position the mouse pointer anywhere in the picture (Figure 1-16).

The mouse pointer changes to a pointing hand.

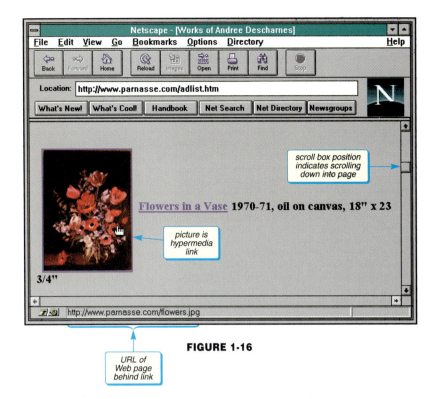

FIGURE 1-16

STEP 7 ▶

Click the picture to display a larger version.

The gray icon in the Stop button on the toolbar changes to red and the status indicator starts into motion, a message appears at the bottom of the screen and the progress indicator moves to the right, both providing information about the progress of the transfer. The picture of the painting starts to display (Figure 1-17).

FIGURE 1-17

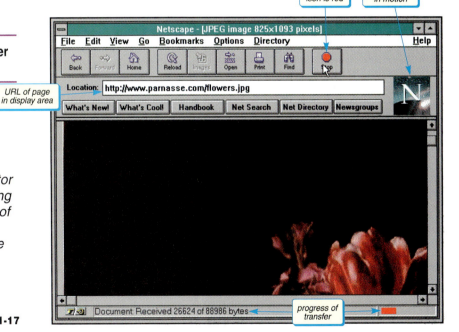

You can see from the preceding steps how simple it is to browse the World Wide Web. Notice also that hypertext links can be words or pictures. Traversing the links is as easy as moving the mouse pointer and clicking the left mouse button.

Stopping the Transfer of a Page

Some pages are very large and will take time to transfer. In addition, after seeing the first portions of a page, you may decide not to wait for the page to finish transferring. Using the **Stop button** on the toolbar, you can stop the ongoing transfer of a page. Recall that while a transfer is in progress, the Stop button icon on the toolbar is red in color. You can stop a transfer only while it is in progress. That means if the Stop button icon is no longer red (returns to gray), the page has been completely received. Therefore, you cannot stop the transfer. Because the Flowers in a Vase picture is fairly large, it could take 30 to 60 seconds to arrive. The following step shows how to interrupt the transfer. Remember, this step will work only if the Stop button icon is still red.

TO STOP A PAGE IN TRANSFER ▼

STEP 1 ▶

Point to the Stop button displaying the red icon ( ) on the toolbar and click.

The Stop button icon changes to gray, and the status indicator motion stops. Any portions of the page that have arrived will display (Figure 1-18).

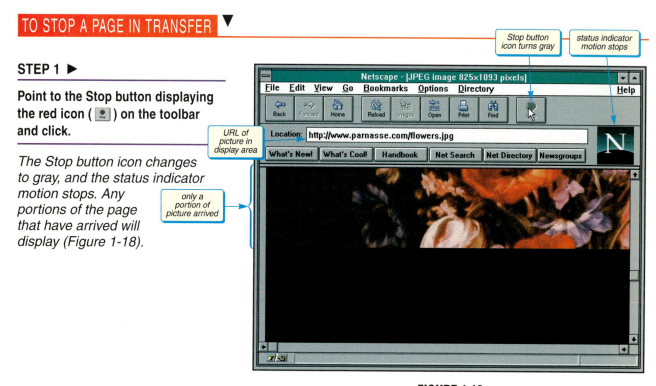

Stop button icon turns gray

status indicator motion stops

URL of picture in display area

only a portion of picture arrived

FIGURE 1-18

A page transfer in progress also can be halted by selecting the Go menu and then choosing the Stop loading command.

Reloading Pages

If you decide you want the complete page transferred, you can reload the page using the **Reload button**, as shown in the following step.

TO RELOAD A PAGE ▼

STEP 1 ▶

Point to the Reload button (🔄) on the toolbar and click.

The Stop button icon on the tool-bar changes to red and the status indicator starts into motion, a message appears in the active link indicator at the bottom of the screen and the progress indicator moves to the right, both providing infor-mation about the pro-gress of the transfer. The picture of the painting starts to display. When the document is done, you can scroll through the picture using the scroll box on the vertical scroll bar (Figure 1-19).

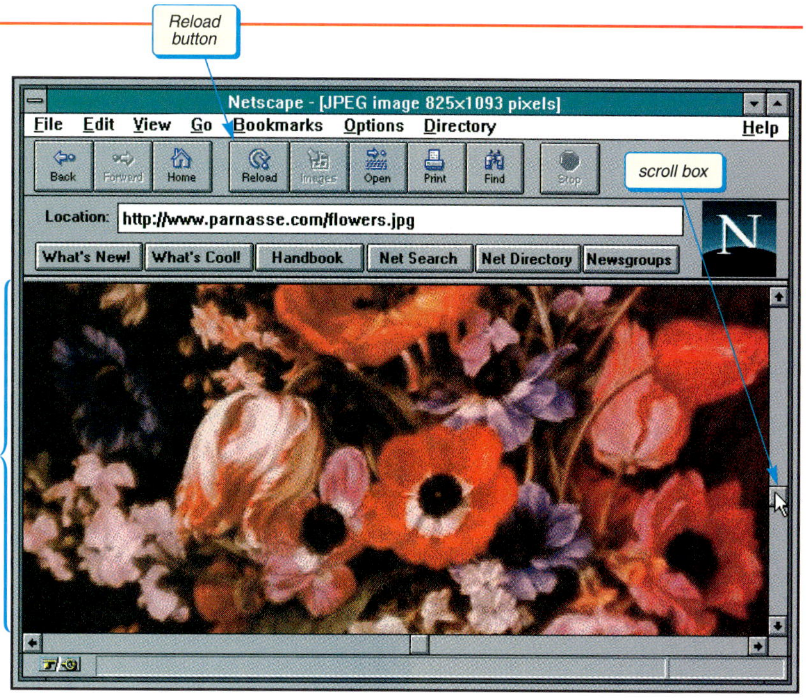

Reload button

complete picture arrived from Web site

scroll box

FIGURE 1-19

If the connection to the Web site where the page is located becomes broken and the page transfer does not finish, you can use the Reload button to request the page again.

Another way to request a page is by clicking in the URL window. An **insertion point** displays, which is the blinking vertical line indicating where the next character you type will appear. By pressing the ENTER key, you will request the page indicated by the URL, or you can type a new URL, requesting a new page to be displayed. Using the steps and techniques just presented, you have learned how to follow hypertext links and browse the World Wide Web.

▶ HISTORY LIST

As you display different Web pages, Netscape keeps track of the ones you visit in a special area called a **history list**. The history list starts out empty every time you start Netscape. The URLs of the pages you display, in the order you visit them, are then stored in the history list by Netscape. You quickly can determine if there are URLs stored in the history list by looking at the **Back button** or the **Forward button** on the toolbar. When Netscape first starts, both buttons are gray, or ghosted, which means they are inactive. As you display pages, the Back button turns to blue. This lets you know that the button is active and URLs of pages you have displayed are stored in the history list.

By using the Back and Forward buttons on the toolbar, you quickly can travel back and forth through the history list redisplaying the pages you have visited. Perform the steps on the next page to move through the history list.

TO MOVE BACK AND FORTH IN THE HISTORY LIST ▼

STEP 1 ▶

Point to the Back button (▣) on the toolbar and click.

The page titled Works of Andree Descharnes redisplays (Figure 1-20). The Forward button on the toolbar changes from gray to blue. This indicates the page displayed is somewhere in the middle of the history list, with URLs behind and in front of the URL of the page currently in the display area. Notice that the Flowers in a Vase link in the display window is no longer blue. It has changed to pink. This is an indication that you previously have visited this link.

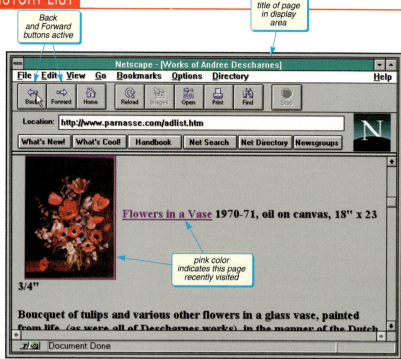

FIGURE 1-20

STEP 2 ▶

Point to the Back button on the toolbar and click.

The page titled Net in Arcadia redisplays (Figure 1-21). You can continue to page backward until you reach the beginning of the history list. At that time, the Back button changes color from blue to gray, indicating that no additional pages to which you can move back are contained in the history list. You can move forward by clicking the Forward button.

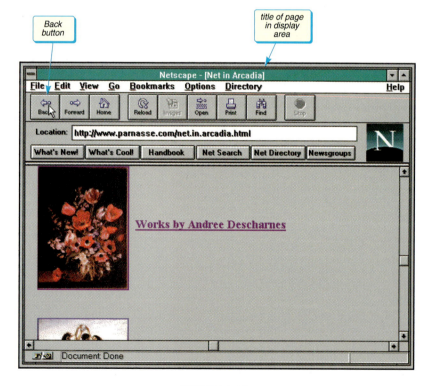

FIGURE 1-21

STEP 3 ►

Point to the Forward button ( ) on the toolbar and click.

The page titled Works of Andree Descharnes redisplays (Figure 1-22).

FIGURE 1-22

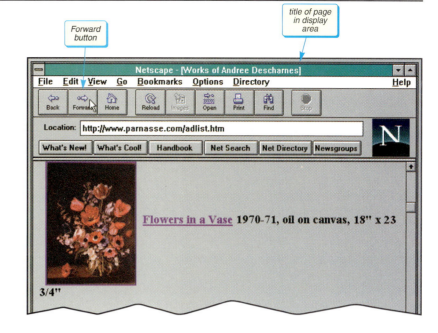

STEP 4 ►

Click the Forward button again.

The JPEG image of the Flowers in a Vase picture redisplays (Figure 1-23). **JPEG** *is a method of encoding pictures on computers.*

FIGURE 1-23

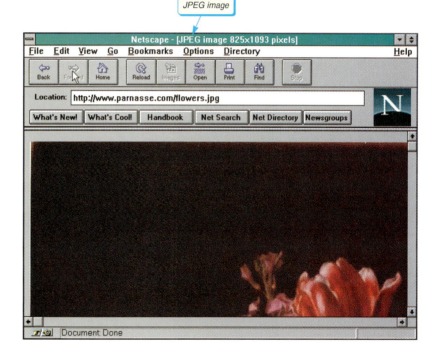

You can see that traversing through the history list is easy using the toolbar buttons.

Displaying a Web Page Using the History List

Using the history list, you can select one of the pages you have visited to redisplay. First, display the entire history list, then move the mouse pointer over the line containing the page title and click the left mouse button as shown in the steps on the next page.

TO DISPLAY A WEB PAGE USING THE HISTORY LIST ▼

STEP 1 ▶

Select the Go menu by clicking Go on the menu bar.

The Go menu displays (Figure 1-24). The titles of the pages you have visited display in the history list, with a check mark next to the currently displayed page.

FIGURE 1-24

STEP 2 ▶

Choose the Works of Andree Descharnes page in the history list by clicking the entry.

The page titled Works of Andree Descharnes redisplays (Figure 1-25).

FIGURE 1-25

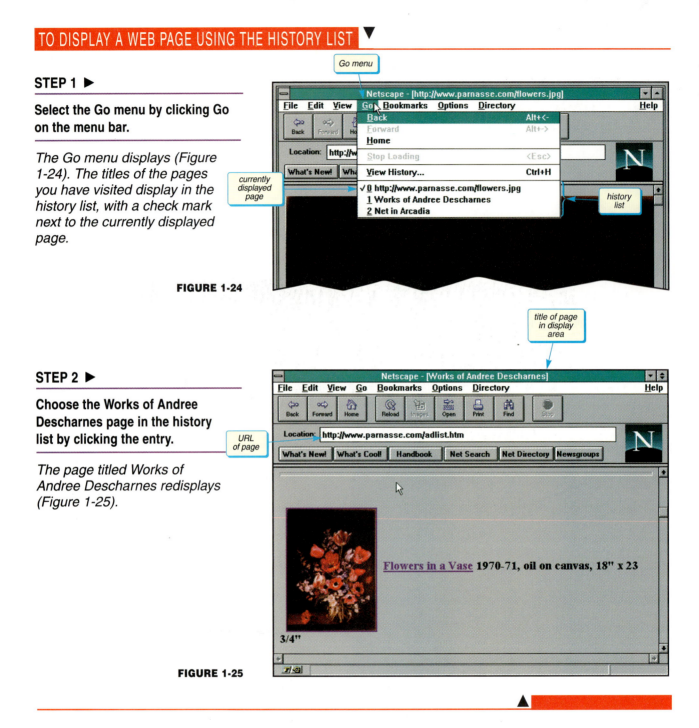

If you have a small history list, it is much easier to use the Back and Forward buttons to traverse the history list than bringing up the history list and selecting pages. If you have visited a large number of Web pages, however, your history list will be long, and it may be easier to use the history list window to select the exact page to redisplay.

History lists are useful for returning to a Web page you have recently visited. Unfortunately, you cannot use the history list to permanently store the URLs of your favorite, or frequently visited, pages. Recall that the history list starts out empty when Netscape starts.

You can see from the previous figures that URLs can be long and cryptic (Figure 1-25). It would be easy to make a mistake while writing down such long, cryptic addresses. Fortunately, Netscape has capabilities for keeping track of your favorite Web pages. You can permanently store the URLs of your favorite pages in an area called a bookmark list.

▶ KEEPING TRACK OF YOUR FAVORITE WEB PAGES

The bookmark feature of Netscape allows you to save the URLs of your favorite Web pages. A **bookmark** consists of the title of the Web page and the URL of that page. Think of the bookmark list as an electronic address book containing the URL and page title of Web pages that are important to you. You can add new bookmarks and remove bookmarks you no longer want. The following steps show how to add the Works of Andree Descharnes URL to the bookmark list.

TO ADD A BOOKMARK TO THE BOOKMARK LIST ▼

STEP 1 ▶

Scroll up to the top of the page. Select the Bookmarks menu.

The Bookmarks menu displays (Figure 1-26). The two commands are Add Bookmark, which adds the current URL to the bookmark list and View Bookmarks, which displays bookmark details. The title portion of any existing bookmarks would appear on the menu after the View Bookmarks command. If this is your first time using Netscape, there probably will be no bookmarks listed, as is the case in Figure 1-26.

STEP 2 ▶

Choose the Add Bookmark command.

The Bookmarks menu disappears. The title of the current page in the display area is added to the end of the bookmark list.

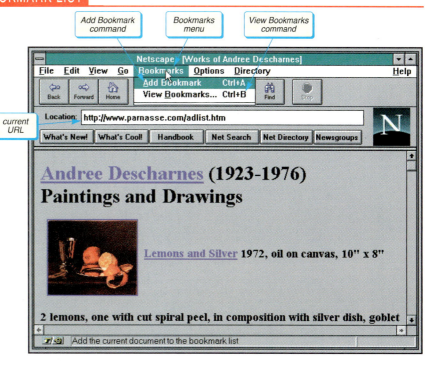

FIGURE 1-26

STEP 3 ▶

Select the Bookmarks menu to verify the page has been added to the bookmark list.

The Bookmarks menu displays, containing the newly added bookmark (Figure 1-27). You may see other bookmarks already added. The bookmark you added should be the last one in the list.

STEP 4 ▶

Close the Bookmarks menu by clicking Bookmarks on the menu bar. Click the Home button (🏠) on the toolbar to redisplay the Netscape home page.

The Bookmarks menu disappears and the Netscape home page displays as shown in Figure 1-28 below.

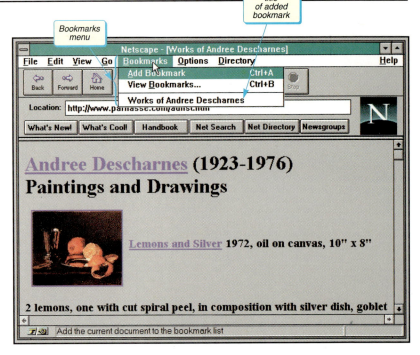

FIGURE 1-27

Other bookmarks you add will be listed below Works of Andree Descharnes. The size of the Bookmarks menu will grow as you add new bookmarks.

Retrieving a Web Page Using a Bookmark

Bookmarks can be used to retrieve the Web page pointed to by the URL associated with the bookmark, as shown in the following steps.

TO RETRIEVE A WEB PAGE USING A BOOKMARK ▼

STEP 1 ▶

Select the Bookmarks menu. Point to the Works of Andree Descharnes bookmark in the list.

The Bookmarks menu displays (Figure 1-28).

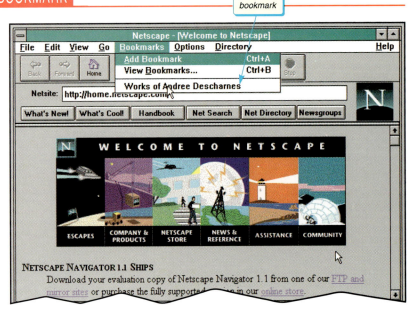

FIGURE 1-28

STEP 2 ▶

Choose the Works of Andree Descharnes bookmark.

The Works of Andree Descharnes page redisplays (Figure 1-29).

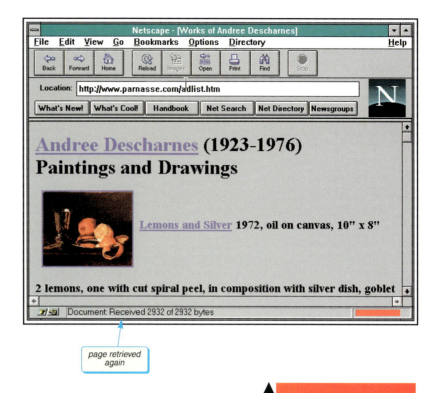

FIGURE 1-29

page retrieved again

You have learned how to add a URL to the bookmark list and how to retrieve that resource using the bookmark list. As you gain experience and continue to browse the World Wide Web, adding pages to your bookmark list, it is likely a time will come when you will want to remove unwanted bookmarks from the list.

Removing Bookmarks

Several reasons exist for wanting to remove a bookmark. With the World Wide Web changing every day, the URL that worked today may not work tomorrow. Perhaps you just do not want a particular bookmark in your list anymore. The following steps show how to remove a bookmark from the bookmark list.

TO REMOVE A BOOKMARK FROM THE BOOKMARK LIST ▼

STEP 1 ▶

Select the Bookmarks menu. Point to the View Bookmarks command.

The Bookmarks menu displays (Figure 1-30).

View Bookmarks command

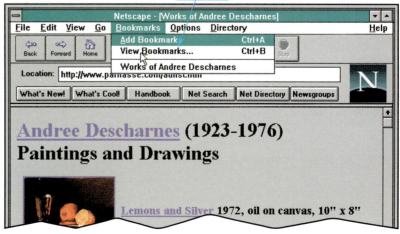

FIGURE 1-30

STEP 2 ►

Choose the View Bookmarks command.

The Bookmark List dialog box displays (Figure 1-31). Notice several buttons in the dialog box. The Add Bookmark button adds the URL of the current page to the bookmark list. The Go To button displays the page with a highlighted bookmark. The Find button searches for a string of characters. The Close button closes the dialog box, the Edit button displays detailed information.

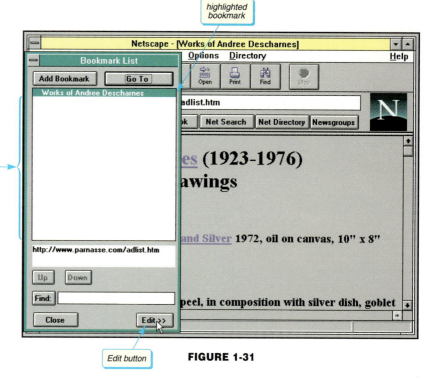

FIGURE 1-31

STEP 3 ►

Click the Edit button in the Bookmark List dialog box. Make sure the Works of Andree Descharnes bookmark is highlighted in the list box. Point to the Remove Item button.

An expanded set of bookmark editing features displays (Figure 1-32). Several new buttons appear, allowing you to perform advanced manipulation of bookmark lists such as reading lists of URLs into Netscape from a diskette file, copying URLs from Netscape on a diskette file, making a copy of a bookmark, changing the attributes of a bookmark, and removing a bookmark.

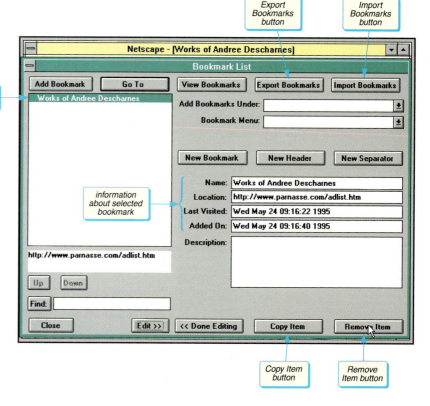

FIGURE 1-32

STEP 4 ▶

Click the Remove Item button.

The Works of Andree Descharnes bookmark disappears (Figure 1-33).

STEP 5 ▶

Click the Close button to close the Bookmark List dialog box.

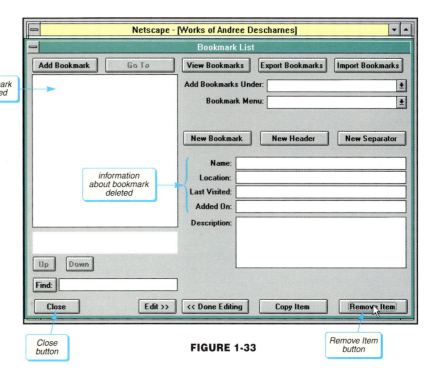

FIGURE 1-33

STEP 6 ▶

To verify that the bookmark has been removed, select the Bookmarks menu.

The Bookmarks menu displays (Figure 1-34). The Works of Andree Descharnes no longer displays.

STEP 7 ▶

Close the Bookmarks menu by clicking Bookmarks on the menu bar.

The Bookmarks menu disappears.

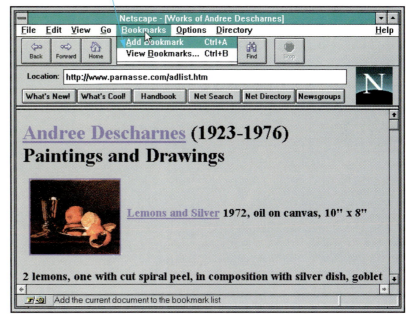

FIGURE 1-34

You have learned how to create, use, and remove bookmarks. Netscape provides many advanced features for handling bookmarks. For example, you can create menus that allow you to organize your bookmark lists into logical categories.

Saving and Restoring Your Bookmark List

Your bookmark list will become an important asset, growing as you add new entries while exploring the World Wide Web. To protect your bookmark list, it is a good idea to save it on a diskette. In addition, if you are using Netscape in an environment where several individuals are using the same computer; for example, in a college computer lab, you need the capability to save and restore your bookmarks so you can reuse them in Netscape.

Saving your bookmark list is accomplished by choosing the View Bookmarks command on the Bookmarks menu. When the Bookmark List dialog box displays, click the Edit button. Click the Export Bookmarks button at the top right in the expanded Bookmark List dialog box (see Figure 1-32 on page N20). The Export Bookmark dialog box displays. In the File Name text box, type a descriptive filename for your list. Then, click the Drives drop-down list box arrow, and select the drive A icon in the Drives drop-down list. Choose the OK button in the Export Bookmark dialog box. Your bookmark list is now saved on a diskette in drive A.

With your bookmark list saved on the diskette, you can now use those bookmarks on any computer running Netscape.

The steps for restoring your bookmarks from the diskette are much the same as for saving bookmarks. Choose the View Bookmarks command on the Bookmarks menu. When the Bookmark List dialog box displays, click the Edit button. Click the Import Bookmarks button at the top right in the expanded Bookmark List dialog box (see Figure 1-32 on page N20). The Import File As dialog box displays. Click the Drives drop-down list box arrow, and select the drive A icon in the Drives drop-down list. In the File Name text box, type the name of your bookmark list. Choose the OK button in the Import File As dialog box. Your bookmarks are added to the end of the current bookmark list.

By saving and importing your bookmark list, you can use your personal collection of bookmarks to access the World Wide Web from any computer on the Internet that is running Netscape.

Saving URLs in the bookmark list is not the only way to save information you obtain using Netscape. Some of the more interesting text and pictures you display while connecting to various Web sites will also be worth saving.

▶ SAVING INFORMATION OBTAINED WITH NETSCAPE

Many different types of Web pages are available on the World Wide Web. Because these pages can help you accumulate information about areas of interest, you may want to save the information you discover for future reference. The different types of Web pages and the different ways you might want to use them, require different ways of saving them. Netscape can save individual pictures, the entire Web page, or selected pieces of the page.

Saving a Web Page

The following steps show how to save the currently displayed Web page on a diskette in drive A.

TO SAVE A WEB PAGE ▼

STEP 1 ▶

Insert a formatted diskette into drive A.

STEP 2 ▶

Select the File menu.

The File menu displays (Figure 1-35).

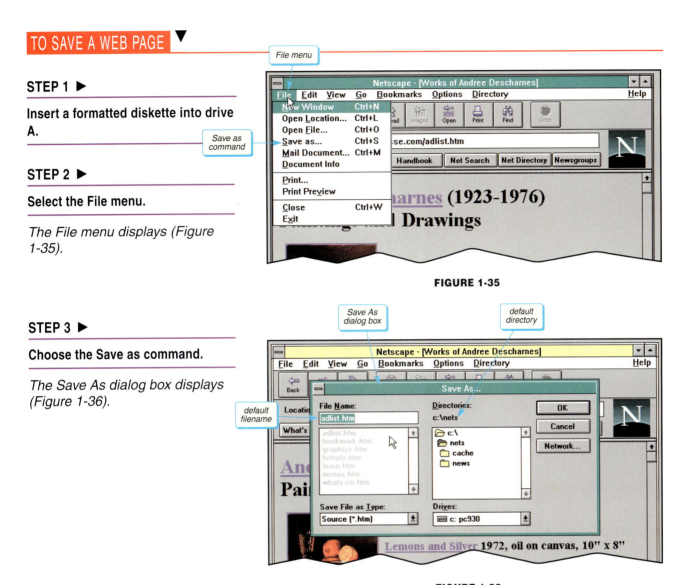

FIGURE 1-35

STEP 3 ▶

Choose the Save as command.

The Save As dialog box displays (Figure 1-36).

FIGURE 1-36

STEP 4 ▶

Type `mypage` in the File Name text box.

The filename mypage replaces adlist.htm (Figure 1-37).

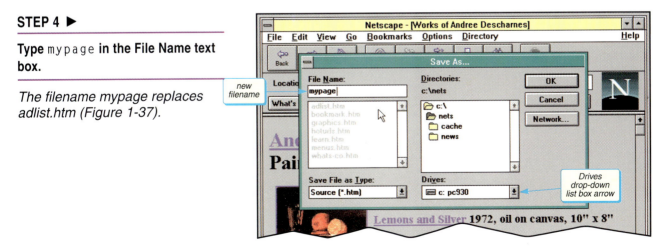

FIGURE 1-37

STEP 5 ▶

Click the Drives drop-down list box arrow.

The Drives drop-down list box displays a list of available drives (Figure 1-38). If the drive A icon does not appear in the Drives drop-down list, use the up scroll arrow on the drop-down list box scroll bar to bring it into view.

FIGURE 1-38

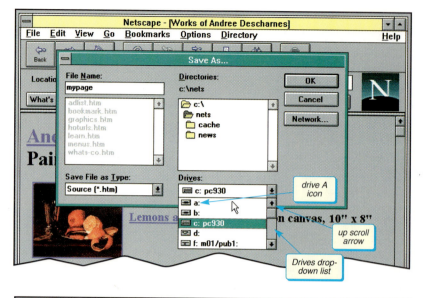

STEP 6 ▶

Select the drive A icon in the Drives drop-down list by clicking the left mouse button. Point to the OK button.

Drive A becomes the selected drive (Figure 1-39).

FIGURE 1-39

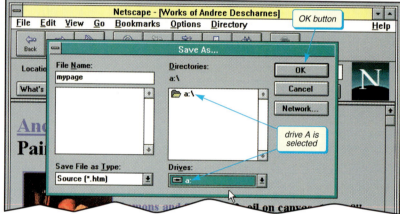

STEP 7 ▶

Choose the OK button in the Save As dialog box.

The Save As dialog box disappears, the page is retrieved again, and is saved on the diskette in drive A using the filename mypage (Figure 1-40).

FIGURE 1-40

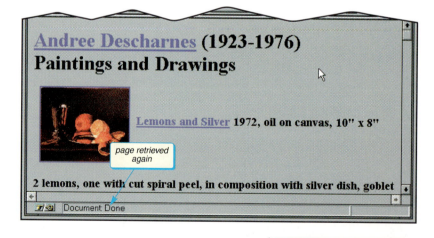

The document is now stored as a regular diskette file and can be opened by any Windows word processor.

Saving a Picture on a Web Page

If you are interested only in the pictures on the page, the following steps illustrate how to save an image on a diskette in drive A.

TO SAVE A PICTURE ON A WEB PAGE ▼

STEP 1 ▶

With the Works of Andree Descharnes page displayed, point to the Lemons and Silver picture. Click the right mouse button. Make sure it is the right mouse button, or you will cause Netscape to retrieve the picture. Point to the Save this Image as command on the pop-up menu.

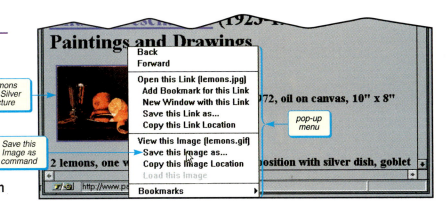

FIGURE 1-41

A pop-up menu of options displays (Figure 1-41).

STEP 2 ▶

Choose the Save this Image as command.

The Save As dialog box displays (Figure 1-42). Drive A is the current drive, because you changed to drive A previously.

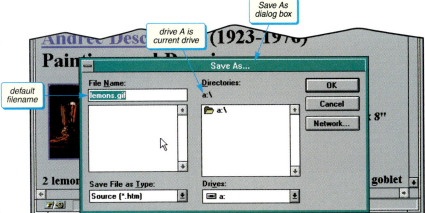

FIGURE 1-42

STEP 3 ▶

Type `mypictr.gif` in the File Name text box.

The filename mypictr.gif replaces lemons.gif (Figure 1-43).

STEP 4 ▶

Choose the OK button in the Save As dialog box.

The Save As dialog box disappears, the picture is retrieved again, and is saved on the diskette in drive A using the filename mypictr.gif.

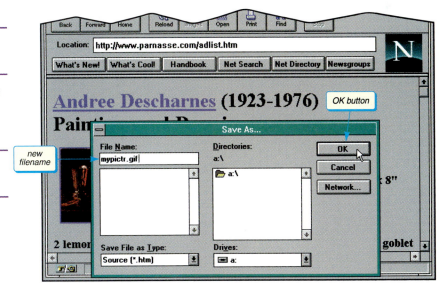

FIGURE 1-43

The picture is now stored as a file on your diskette and can be displayed with image viewers such as Paintbrush or a Windows word processor. The last technique for saving information uses the Clipboard to insert portions of a Web page into a Notepad file. **Notepad** is a text editor provided with Microsoft Windows.

▶ COPYING AND PASTING USING THE CLIPBOARD

Portions of, or even an entire, Web page can be inserted into another Windows application, such as Notepad, using copy and paste facilities. The portion of the Web page you select will be placed on the Clipboard and then can be inserted into another application. The **Clipboard** is a temporary storage area in main memory. Information you cut or copy on the Clipboard remains there until you change it or clear it.

To start the operation, you will display Program Manager and start Microsoft Notepad. Next, you must switch back to Netscape and copy to the Clipboard the portion of the text you want to paste in the Notepad document. Finally, you will switch back to Notepad and paste the contents from the Clipboard into the document. These steps are shown in the following sections.

Starting Notepad

To start Notepad, the Windows Program Manager must display on the screen and the Microsoft Accessories group window must be open. Once Notepad is started and the appropriate document is opened, switch to Netscape as shown in the following steps.

TO START NOTEPAD ▼

STEP 1 ▶

Hold down the ALT key. While holding down the ALT key, press the TAB key until the box titled Program Manager displays in the middle of the screen. Release both keys.

Windows displays Program Manager (Figure 1-44).

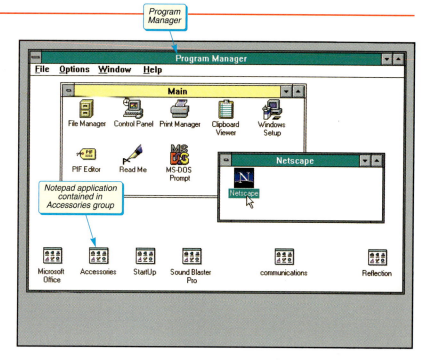

FIGURE 1-44

STEP 2 ▶

Point to the Accessories group icon and double-click the left mouse button.

The Accessories group window displays (Figure 1-45).

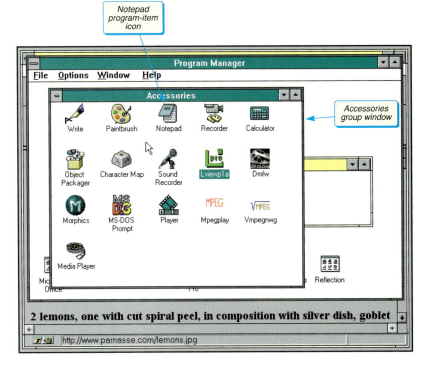

FIGURE 1-45

STEP 3 ▶

Point to the Notepad program-item icon and double-click the left mouse button.

The Notepad window displays (Figure 1-46).

STEP 4 ▶

Hold down the ALT key. While holding down the ALT key, press the TAB key until the box titled Netscape displays in the middle of the screen. Release both keys.

The Netscape window will display.

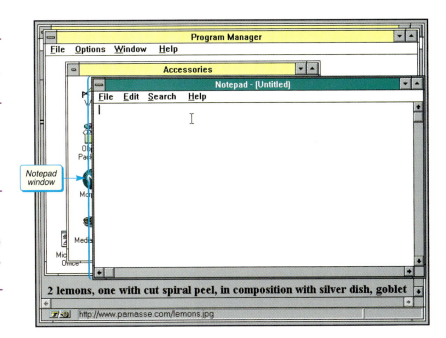

FIGURE 1-46

With the Notepad application started, the next step is to complete the copy and paste operation.

Copying Text from a Web Page and Pasting It in Notepad

The following steps show how to copy a paragraph of text from the biography of Andree Descharnes to the Clipboard, switch to Notepad, and paste the paragraph on the Clipboard into the Notepad document.

TO COPY AND PASTE A SECTION OF A WEB PAGE INTO NOTEPAD ▼

STEP 1 ▶

Point to the blue Andree Descharnes text.

The mouse pointer changes to a pointing hand, indicating the Andree Descharnes text is a link (Figure 1-47).

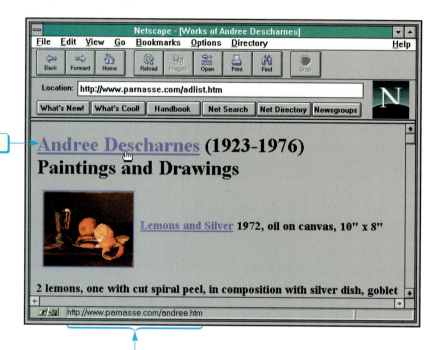

FIGURE 1-47

STEP 2 ▶

Click the Andree Descharnes text.

Because the Andree Descharnes text is a link to the Andree Descharnes Biography Web page, that Web page displays on the screen (Figure 1-48).

STEP 3 ▶

Point to the beginning of the text in the first paragraph.

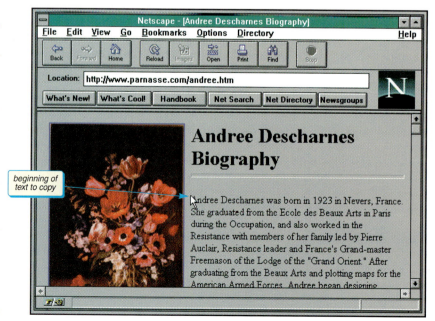

FIGURE 1-48

STEP 4 ►

Hold down the left mouse button and drag the mouse pointer to the end of the second sentence, and then release the mouse button.

The selected text is highlighted (Figure 1-49).

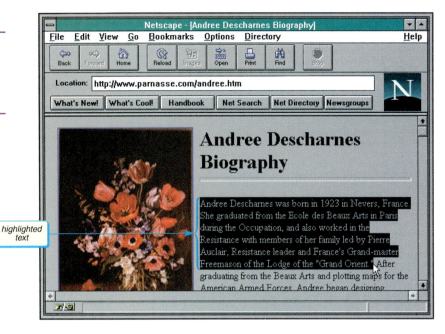

FIGURE 1-49

STEP 5 ►

Select the Edit menu. Point to the Copy command.

The Edit menu displays and the mouse pointer points to the Copy command (Figure 1-50).

STEP 6 ►

Choose the Copy command.

The Edit menu closes and the selected text is copied to the Clipboard.

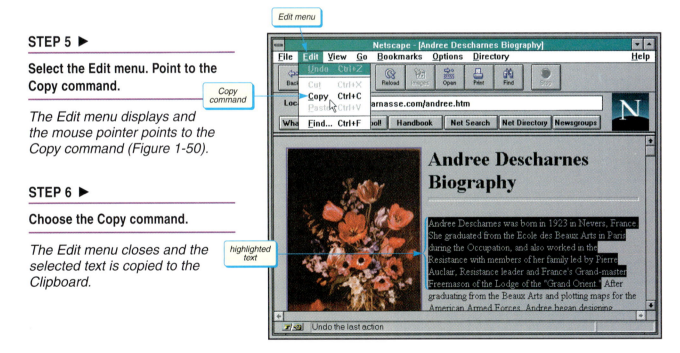

FIGURE 1-50

STEP 7 ▶

Hold down the ALT key. While holding down the ALT key, press the TAB key until the box titled Notepad displays in the middle of the screen. Release both keys.

Windows displays the Notepad window.

STEP 8 ▶

Select Edit menu.

The Edit menu displays (Figure 1-51).

FIGURE 1-51

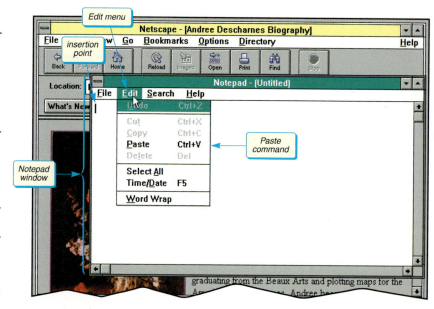

STEP 9 ▶

Choose the Paste command.

The contents of the Clipboard are pasted in the Notepad window beginning at the location of the insertion point (Figure 1-52). Notice the spaces beginning at lines 2 through 6 that allow for the picture to appear in the Web page just pasted. These spaces are to be removed.

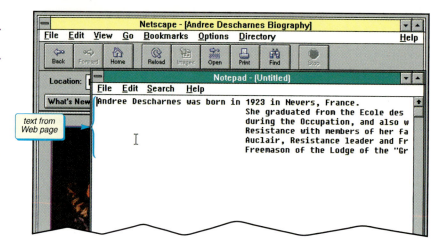

FIGURE 1-52

STEP 10 ▶

Using the DELETE key, remove the spaces at the beginning of lines 2 through 6.

The document lines up to the left (Figure 1-53).

FIGURE 1-53

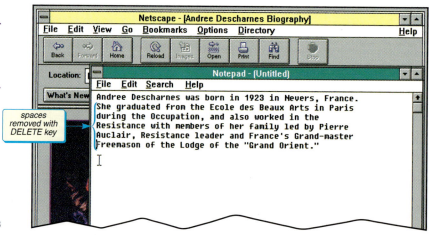

The copy and paste operation is complete. The Notepad document contains a paragraph of text you retrieved from the World Wide Web.

Saving the Notepad Document

When you are finished with the Notepad document, you can save it on a diskette and exit Notepad, as shown in the following steps.

TO SAVE THE NOTEPAD DOCUMENT AND EXIT NOTEPAD

STEP 1 ▶

Select the File menu and choose the Save as command.

The Save As dialog box displays (Figure 1-54).

FIGURE 1-54

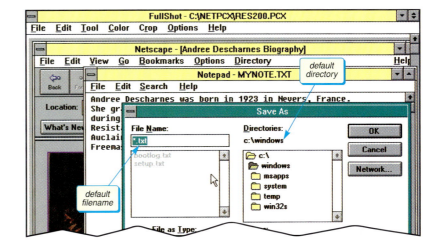

STEP 2 ▶

Type `mynote.txt` **in the File Name text box.**

The filename mynote.txt replaces the default filename (*.txt) (Figure 1-55).

FIGURE 1-55

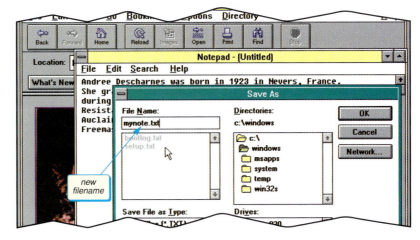

STEP 3 ▶

Click the Drives drop-down list box arrow.

The Drives drop-down list box displays a list of available drives (Figure 1-56). If the drive A icon does not appear in the Drives drop-down list, use the up scroll arrow on the drop-down list box scroll bar to bring it into view.

FIGURE 1-56

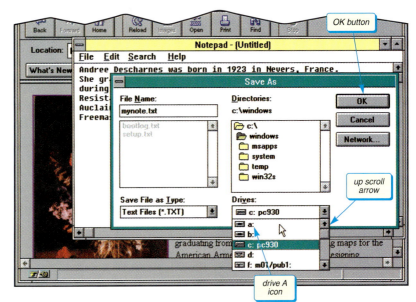

STEP 4 ▶

Select drive A. Choose the OK button in the Save As dialog box. Point to the Control-menu box in Notepad.

The Save As dialog box disappears (Figure 1-57), and the Notepad file is saved on the diskette in drive A.

STEP 5 ▶

Double-click Notepad's Control-menu box to close Notepad.

Notepad closes, and the Netscape window will redisplay.

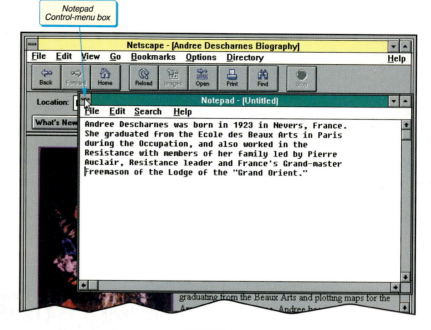

FIGURE 1-57

In the previous steps, you pasted into Notepad. Using the same techniques, you can also paste into any Windows application on your computer.

You have learned how to save information you retrieve from a Web site. In addition to saving, Netscape allows you to print the pages you find interesting as you travel around the Web.

▶ PRINTING A WEB PAGE IN NETSCAPE

Netscape printing capabilities allow you to print both the text and graphic portions of a Web page. The easiest way to print is to use the **Print button** on the toolbar. The following steps print the current Web page, Andree Descharnes Biography.

TO PRINT A WEB PAGE ▼

STEP 1 ▶

Ready the printer according to the printer instructions.

STEP 2 ▶

Point to the Print button (🖨) on the toolbar and click.

The Print dialog box displays (Figure 1-58). The All option button is selected in the Print Range area.

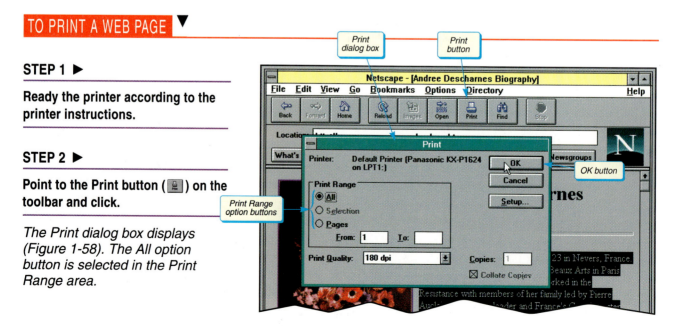

FIGURE 1-58

STEP 3 ▶

Choose the OK button in the Print dialog box to print the entire Web page.

The Netscape dialog box displays indicating the printing status (Figure 1-59). When the document has been sent to the printer, the dialog box disappears, returning control to the Netscape window.

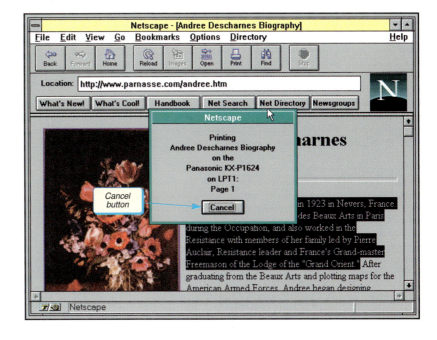

FIGURE 1-59

STEP 4 ▶

When the printer stops, retrieve the printout (Figure 1-60).

Andree Descharnes Biography

Andree Descharnes was born in 1923 in Nevers, France. She graduated from the Ecole des Beaux Arts in Paris during the Occupation, and also worked in the Resistance with members of her family led by Pierre Auclair, Resistance leader and France's Grand-master Freemason of the Lodge of the "Grand Orient." After graduating from the Beaux Arts and plotting maps for the American Armed Forces, Andree began designing wallpaper and fabric. But it is in Floral and Still-life painting that she truly excelled and to which she eventually devoted every spare moment of her time. A classicist in the tradition of Poussin and Chardin, Descharnes also followed Montaigne's "Juste Milieu" philosophy of subtle intelligence and grace. The truth she uncovered in the simple objects she depicted has a zen like immediacy captured with an almost miraculous brushwork. When celebrated art historian Argan saw one of Descharnes paintings in her and spouse Alfred Russell's apartment in Trastevere, he was convinced it was a seventeenth century Dutch Masterpiece. Andree Descharnes and Alfred Russell met when he had his first Paris exhibit as a central figure in the group of abstract expressionists who worked in both Paris and New York. The two were married in 1949 with Ad Reinhardt serving as best man. During the early fifties, Descharnes concentrated on pen and ink drawings and watercolors of the world around her, such as the breakfast table or the views out the window of the Paris apartment, all done in a nervous "Giacometti style." In the mid fifties Alfred Russell began copying masterpieces in the Louvre. This period proved a turning point in both artists' careers. For Alfred Russell it spawned a renewed interest in the classical tradition of the past, not only in the paintings of sixteenth and seventeenth centuries, but also in the sculpture and philosophy of the Greeks and in the use of the Figure as an Abstract language. In 1956 Alfred Russell and Andree Descharnes had a daughter, Elsie, while they were living in Surrealist painter Kurt Seligmann's "Villa Seurat," an early Modernist House in Paris's 14th arrondissement, as Alfred Russell was on sabbatical from his teaching job at Brooklyn College. Andree did not start painting still-lives until seven years later, when her childcare and textile design duties became less demanding. While the family spent much of 1961 living in Nice, France, Andree started a series of floral paintings, with the beautiful roses that grew in the enclosed garden behind the house. Several of these paintings are on view in the museum. She went on to paint a variety of still-life subjects, always emphasizing the living elements within a formal compositional structure, for instance, one lemon amidst an arrangement of reflective silver objects. Andree Descharnes died prematurely in 1976 after a long battle with cancer. Much of her small but exquisite oeuvre of oil paintings and drawings is on exhibit here.

FIGURE 1-60

Notice the printing options in the Print dialog box in Figure 1-58. You can print the entire document, a portion of the document, or selected pages of the document. The resolution of the output can be adjusted. Multiple copies of what you print can be selected. Printer settings can be changed, and the printing request can be canceled, returning you to the Netscape window. The Cancel button in the Netscape dialog box (Figure 1-59) allows you to cancel the print request. You can also print a Web page by selecting the File menu and choosing the Print command.

Although most Web pages are for viewing, other documents are interactive. You can enter and send text to other sites using special data entry forms, as described in the next section.

▶ WEBCHAT

N etscape does more than just display Web pages. You can also write on certain types of pages and send your comments over the Internet. These special pages can contain **forms** in which you type information, such as a name and address. The form usually contains a button you click to send the information back to the Web site from which the page originated. Check boxes, option buttons, menus, selection lists, and a command button to clear the information you enter all may be included on a form.

You can use the forms for entering information to query databases, order merchandise, send electronic mail, post news group articles, fill out surveys, and communicate with other Internet users. To demonstrate how to use Netscape forms, the following steps show you how to engage in live conversations using a World Wide Web service called WebChat.

Conversing Over the Internet Using WebChat

WebChat allows you to engage in live, ongoing conversations with other participants on the Internet. WebChat is like a computerized party-line, with everyone reading other people's comments and typing their own comments for everyone else to see, all in the time it takes to redisplay a Web page. WebChat can have hundreds of people all trying to converse at the same time. The WebChat page will contain a number of the most recent comments from the active WebChat participants. As new comments appear, old ones are removed.

Connecting to a WebChat Session

The following steps show how to connect to the WebChat service at the Internet Roundtable Society. Because WebChat uses Web pages for communication, you are required to supply the URL of the WebChat Web site.

TO CONNECT TO A WEBCHAT SESSION ▼

STEP 1 ▶

Drag the mouse pointer over the URL in the URL window.

The URL is highlighted (Figure 1-61).

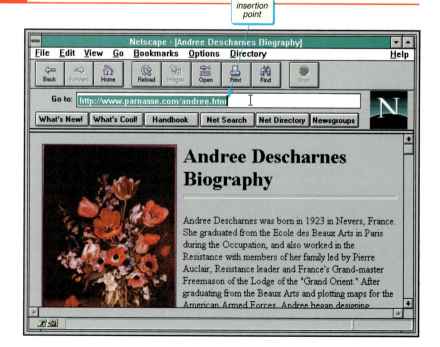

FIGURE 1-61

STEP 2 ▶

Type http://www
.irsociety.com/webchat
.html **(Figure 1-62).**

FIGURE 1-62

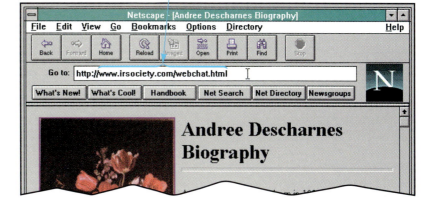

STEP 3 ▶

Press the ENTER key.

The Welcome to WebChat page displays (Figure 1-63). The page contains information about WebChat. The entry point to live conversations is further down the page.

FIGURE 1-63

STEP 4 ▶

Using the scroll box on the vertical scroll bar on the right side of the display area, scroll down the page until the white WebChat entry button ( ) displays (Figure 1-64).

FIGURE 1-64

STEP 5 ▶

Click the WebChat entry button. Point to the Click here to enter WebChat button
([Click here to enter WebChat]).

The WebChat page displays (Figure 1-65). The WebChat page contains information about where to send comments about WebChat.

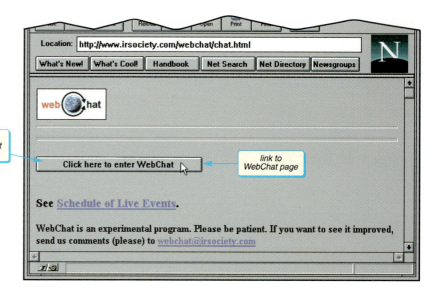

FIGURE 1-65

STEP 6 ▶

Click the Click here to enter Webchat button, and then point to the Continue button.

The Security Information dialog box displays, informing you that what you send over the Internet will not be secure and warning you that someone could see the information you are sending (Figure 1-66). It is not a good idea to send passwords, account numbers, or other personal or confidential information using WebChat.

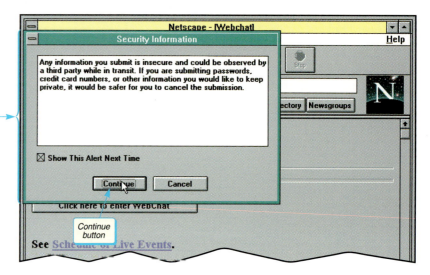

FIGURE 1-66

STEP 7 ▶

Click the Continue button.

The Main Hallway chat page displays (Figure 1-67).

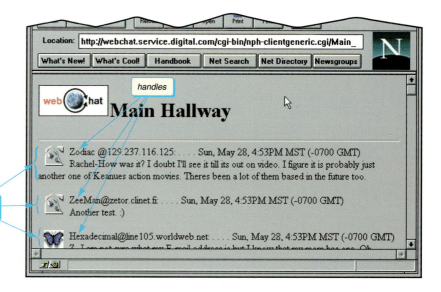

FIGURE 1-67

STEP 8 ▶

Scroll down until you see the input form shown in Figure 1-68.

It is on this portion of the Web page where you enter a name to identify yourself and a comment to add to the ongoing WebChat conversation.

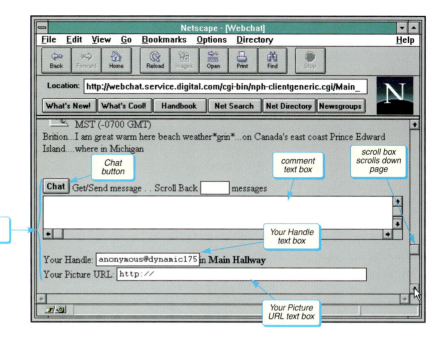

FIGURE 1-68

▲

The chat page is made up of two parts. The first part contains the comments from the chat participants in the order they arrived, with the oldest comments at the top and the newest comments toward the bottom of the page. Each comment is made up of a handle, the date and time, and the actual text of the comment. A **handle** is the name by which participants identify themselves. In Figure 1-67, the handles Zodiac, ZeeMan, and Hexadecimal are shown.

The second part of the page, at the bottom, contains the form where you will enter your comments and request that the page be updated with fresh comments. You must redisplay the WebChat page to see fresh comments because the page is actually a snapshot of the comments that existed at the time you requested the page when clicking the Click here to enter WebChat button, as shown in Figure 1-65. As comments are sent by participants, they are added to the bottom of the page.

Displaying New WebChat Comments

The bottom of the WebChat page contains the form where you request an updated page of comments. The steps on the next page illustrate how to request a fresh page of comments.

TO DISPLAY NEW WEBCHAT COMMENTS ▼

STEP 1 ▶

Click the Chat button (Chat).

The Security Information dialog box displays (Figure 1-69). The Show This Alert Next Time check box is selected. This dialog box will continue to display each time you request a fresh page of comments or send a comment of your own. You can turn off the display of the dialog box.

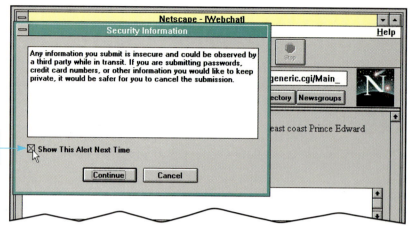

FIGURE 1-69

STEP 2 ▶

Click the Show This Alert Next Time check box in the Security Information dialog box.

The x in the box disappears, indicating the message will not display again (Figure 1-70).

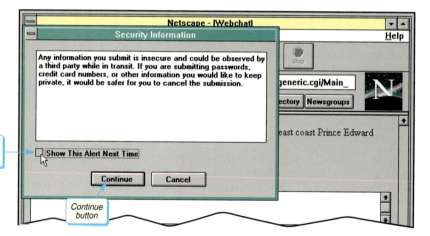

FIGURE 1-70

STEP 3 ▶

Click the Continue button in the Security Information dialog box.

An updated chat page with new comments displays (Figure 1-71).

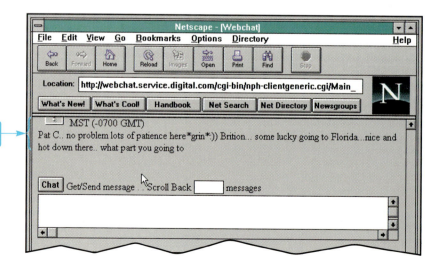

FIGURE 1-71

To obtain new comments, repeatedly click the Chat button in the WebChat page. The page will redisplay. Not only is reading other people's conversations fun, but you also can participate in those conversations.

Participating in WebChat Conversations

Before engaging in conversations, you should identify yourself to permit other chat participants to distinguish which pieces of the conversation are from you. You can choose a name by which your pieces of conversation will be recognized by typing a handle that is entered in a special box in the form. A handle can be your real name or perhaps some word that describes your personality.

When you first bring up the WebChat page, a default handle, anonymous, appears in the handle box. Choose a handle and type it in the handle box over the word anonymous, as shown in the following steps.

TO ENTER A CHAT HANDLE ▼

STEP 1 ▶

With the bottom of the WebChat page displayed, point to the left of the word anonymous in the Your Handle text box and click the left mouse button.

An insertion point appears to the left of the word anonymous (Figure 1-72).

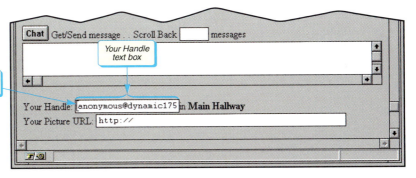

FIGURE 1-72

STEP 2 ▶

Use the DELETE key to delete the word anonymous. Type your first name.

Your first name displays in the Your Handle text box. In Figure 1-73, the first name of Kurt Jordan displays.

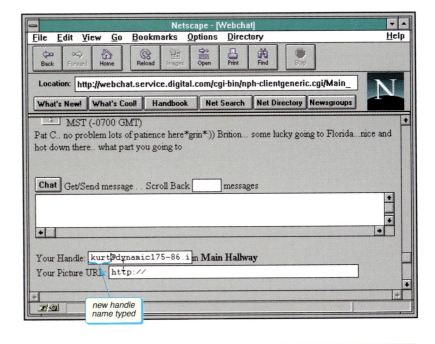

FIGURE 1-73

Notice in Figure 1-67 on page N36, that some people have pictures next to their comments on the WebChat page. Pictures can be selected from a library of pictures available from the WebChat page. The Picture library link at the bottom of the WebChat page will display pictures from which you can select to identify your comments. Other participants are able to find your comments by looking for your picture, instead of having to read the handle on every comment on the chat page to identify you.

Having entered your handle, you now can join in the conversations on the chat page, as shown in the following steps.

TO CONVERSE ON WEBCHAT ▼

STEP 1 ▶

With the bottom of the WebChat page displayed, point to the comment text box and click the left mouse button.

An insertion point displays in the top left corner of the comment text box (Figure 1-74).

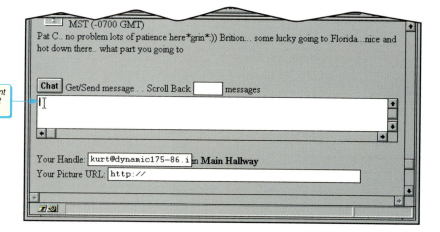

FIGURE 1-74

STEP 2 ▶

Type a message that identifies who you are and where you are located, such as the message shown in Figure 1-75.

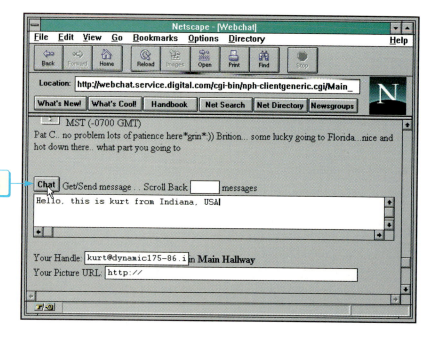

FIGURE 1-75

STEP 3 ▶

Click the Chat button.

The chat page redisplays with your comment inserted on the page (Figure 1-76). Participants now can see your comment. Other people's comments will be placed below yours. Recall, you have to reload the page to see the new comments by clicking the Chat button.

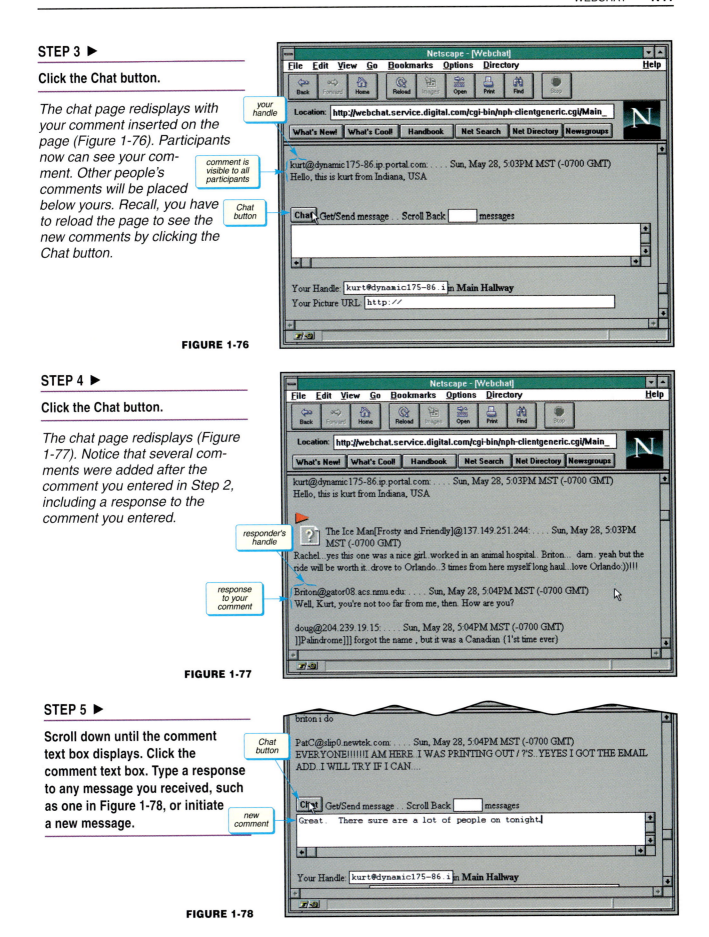

FIGURE 1-76

STEP 4 ▶

Click the Chat button.

The chat page redisplays (Figure 1-77). Notice that several comments were added after the comment you entered in Step 2, including a response to the comment you entered.

FIGURE 1-77

STEP 5 ▶

Scroll down until the comment text box displays. Click the comment text box. Type a response to any message you received, such as one in Figure 1-78, or initiate a new message.

FIGURE 1-78

STEP 6 ▶

Click the Chat button.

The chat page redisplays with your comment inserted on the page (Figure 1-79).

comment is visible to all participants

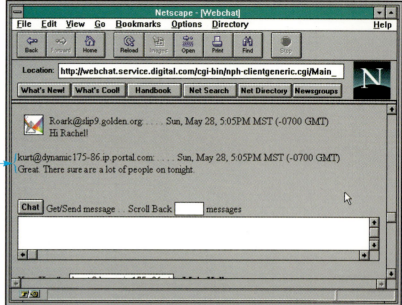

FIGURE 1-79

STEP 7 ▶

Click the Chat button again.

The chat page redisplays (Figure 1-80). You can continue the conversation in this manner, reading what other people have to say, and entering your own comments.

your comment

latest comments

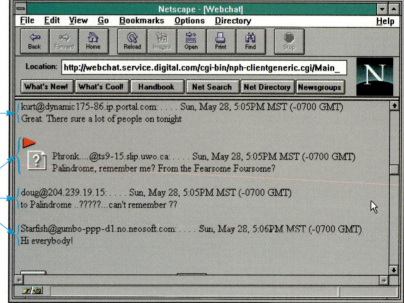

FIGURE 1-80

Using the techniques and steps just presented, you have successfully participated in WebChat conversations. If you have trouble following the dialog, do not be discouraged. Hundreds of people may be trying to talk all at the same time. WebChat displays the lines people type in the order they are received, making it difficult to follow what one person types because the comments are interspersed with comments from other people who are trying to have their own conversations.

As you continue to participate in WebChat, you will get better at deciphering this nonsequential method of conversation. Be aware. WebChat is totally unregulated. People can say whatever they please, including things that may be offensive.

▶ NETSCAPE ONLINE HELP

Netscape is a robust program with many features and options. Although you will quickly master some of these features and options, it is not necessary for you to remember everything about each one of them. Reference materials and other forms of assistance are available from within Netscape. You can retrieve these materials and use the methods previously discussed to print them or save them on a diskette. The following steps show how to obtain information about printing from Netscape.

TO GET HELP IN NETSCAPE ▼

STEP 1 ▶

Select the Help menu. Point to the Handbook command.

The Help menu displays (Figure 1-81).

FIGURE 1-81

STEP 2 ▶

Choose Handbook on the Help menu. Using the scroll box on the scroll bar, scroll down the page.

The Netscape Online Handbook page displays (Figure 1-82). The handbook contains hypermedia links to useful, informative documents such as Internet basics, a brief tutorial of Netscape, and other reference materials. An alphabetical Index displays near the bottom of the page. Information about printing will be found under the letter P.

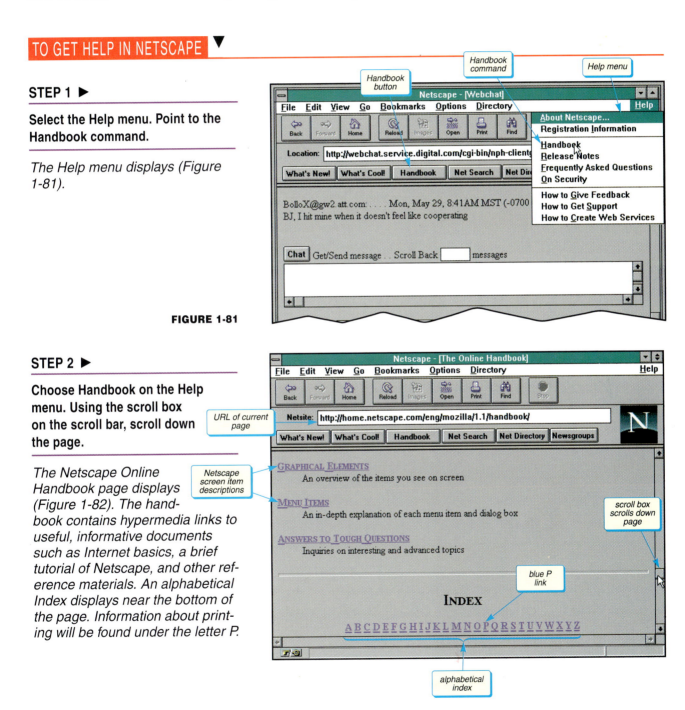

FIGURE 1-82

STEP 3 ▶

Point to the blue P link and click the left mouse button.

A page displays with help links to topics beginning with the letter P (Figure 1-83).

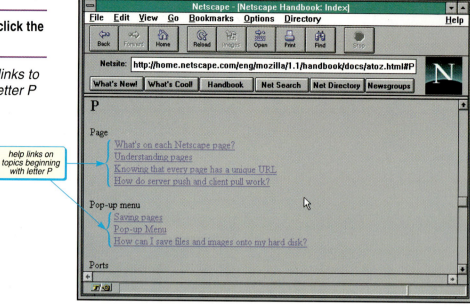

FIGURE 1-83

STEP 4 ▶

Using the scroll box on the vertical scroll bar, scroll down the page until Print commands display (Figure 1-84).

General topics from which to choose display on the screen (Figure 1-84). The Print commands topic contains information on printing.

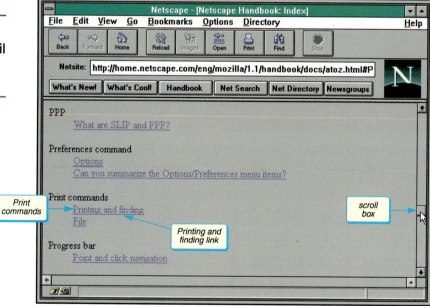

FIGURE 1-84

STEP 5 ▶

Click the Printing and finding text.

Information on printing and finding displays because the Printing and finding text was linked to the Printing and finding Web page (Figure 1-85).

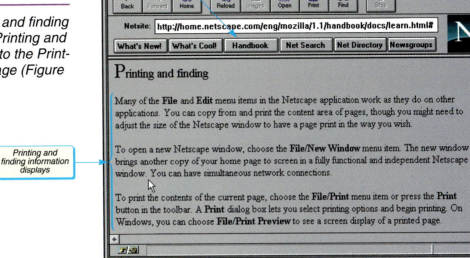

Handbook button

Printing and finding information displays

FIGURE 1-85

You can return to the Index using the Back button on the toolbar and search the alphabetical index for other topics of interest.

The previous steps used the Handbook command on the Help menu to obtain help. You can also click the Handbook directory button (Handbook) below the URL window. Table 1-1 summarizes the commands on the Help menu shown in Figure 1-81 on page N43.

▶ **TABLE 1-1**

MENU COMMAND	FUNCTION
About Netscape	Displays information about the Netscape program
Registration Information	Displays information about registering Netscape
Handbook	Displays menus of help topics
Release Notes	Displays information about the current release of Netscape
Frequently Asked Questions	Displays the answers to frequently asked questions
On Security	Displays information about sending secured information over the Internet
How to Give Feedback	Describes how to send mail to the Netscape Communications Corporation
How to Get Support	Describes how to obtain technical support
How to Create Web Services	Describes how to create your own Web site

▶ EXITING NETSCAPE

After you have browsed the World Wide Web and learned how to manage Web pages, Project 1 is complete. To exit Netscape and return control to Program Manager, perform the following steps.

TO EXIT NETSCAPE ▼

STEP 1 ▶

Point to the Control-menu box in the title bar (Figure 1-86).

STEP 2 ▶

Double-click the left mouse button.

The Program Manager window will redisplay.

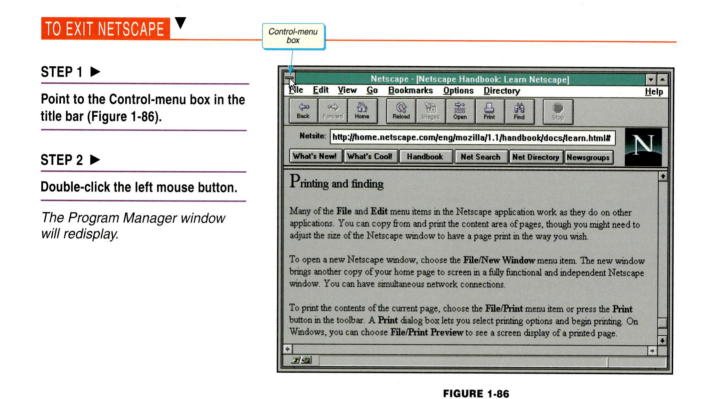

FIGURE 1-86

Instead of double-clicking the Control-menu box in the title bar, you can also quit Netscape by choosing the Exit command on the File menu.

▶ PROJECT SUMMARY

In this project, you learned about the Internet, the World Wide Web, and URLs. You learned how to follow hypertext links and display Web pages. Then, you learned how to use Netscape's history list and how to create and use bookmarks. Saving and printing images and Web pages were presented. Using the techniques and steps presented, you conversed with participants of WebChat. Finally, you learned how to use Netscape's online Help facility.

▶ ## KEY TERMS AND INDEX

active link indicator *(N7)*
Back button *(N13)*
bookmark *(N17)*
browser *(N4)*
Clipboard *(N26)*
directory button *(N6)*
display area *(N5)*
domain name *(N7)*
file specification *(N7)*
forms *(N34)*
Forward button *(N13)*
handle *(N37)*
history list *(N13)*
home page *(N4)*

hypermedia *(N3)*
hypertext link *(N2)*
HTTP (hypertext transport protocol) *(N7)*
insertion point *(N13)*
Internet *(N2)*
JPEG *(N15)*
link *(N3)*
menu bar *(N6)*
network *(N2)*
Notepad *(N26)*
path *(N7)*
Print button *(N32)*
progress indicator *(N7)*

protocol *(N7)*
Reload button *(N12)*
status indicator *(N7)*
Stop button *(N12)*
title bar *(N5)*
toolbar *(N6)*
URL (Universal Resource Locator) *(N7)*
URL window *(N7)*
WebChat *(N34)*
Web page *(N3)*
Web site *(N3)*
World Wide Web (WWW) *(N3)*

S T U D E N T   A S S I G N M E N T S

STUDENT ASSIGNMENT 1
True/False

Instructions: Circle T if the statement is true or F if the statement is false.

T F 1. Thousands of new users are coming online on the Internet every month.
T F 2. One or more computer systems, terminals, and communications technologies connected together is called a link.
T F 3. Hypermedia is accessed by clicking certain words or pictures designated as links.
T F 4. Home pages are usually bland, uninteresting indexes to information.
T F 5. Browsers relieve you from having to remember the syntax of complex commands needed to connect to computers on the Internet.
T F 6. The title of the current page in the Netscape display area is shown in the URL window.
T F 7. Each menu name on the menu bar contains a drop-down menu of commands.
T F 8. A typical URL (Universal Resource Locator) is composed of two parts, a title and hypermedia address.
T F 9. The domain name is the Internet address of a computer on the Internet.
T F 10. The active link indicator and the status indicator each serve more than one purpose.
T F 11. Links you find one day in the What's New and What's Cool pages may not be there the next day.
T F 12. Hypertext links on a Web page cannot be readily identified.
T F 13. To select a hypertext link to follow, you must point to the link and click the left mouse button.
T F 14. You can halt the transfer of a Web page by clicking the gray Stop button on the toolbar.
T F 15. The history list provides a permanent record of the Web pages you visit.
T F 16. The Back and Forward buttons are used to traverse through the bookmark list.
T F 17. URLs can be removed from the bookmark list.
T F 18. You can save the text portion of Web pages, but not the pictures.
T F 19. The Clipboard can be used to transfer portions of Web documents to other Windows applications.
T F 20. Special forms on Web pages allow you to send information over the Internet.

STUDENT ASSIGNMENT 2
Multiple Choice

Instructions: Circle the correct answer.

1. The collection of hypertext links throughout the Internet create an interconnected network of links called the _____.
   a. World Hypermedia Network
   b. Information Superhighway
   c. World Wide Web
   d. World InternetWork

2. The starting point for most Web sites is called a _____.
   a. browser
   b. URL
   c. root directory
   d. home page

3. An item that is *not* part of the Netscape window is a _____.
   a. menu bar
   b. format button
   c. toolbar
   d. status indicator

4. The address of Web pages at Web sites on the World Wide Web is called a _____.
   a. Universal Resource Locator
   b. Internet address
   c. domain name
   d. path

5. You can identify a hypertext link because _____.
   a. the link is in reverse video
   b. the computer beeps when the pointer is moved over the link
   c. the color of the link changes when the mouse pointer is moved over it
   d. the mouse pointer changes to a pointing hand when moved over the link

6. If you want a fresh copy of the Web page in the display area, click the _____.
   a. red Stop button on the toolbar
   b. Reload button on the toolbar
   c. Back button on the toolbar
   d. status indicator containing the Netscape corporate logo

7. The Netscape menu that allows you to retrieve permanently stored URLs is called _____.
   a. Bookmarks
   b. Go
   c. View
   d. File

8. To print a Web page, either use the Print command on the File menu or click the _____ button.
   a. Find
   b. What's Cool
   c. Print
   d. Reload

9. To retrieve a fresh copy of a form being used for live conversations, _____.
   a. click the Print button on the toolbar
   b. press the ALT + TAB keys
   c. click the Forward button on the toolbar
   d. click the specially designated button on the form
10. Documents containing topics such as Internet basics, a Netscape tutorial, and an alphabetical index can be found by _____.
   a. choosing the File menu on the menu bar
   b. clicking the Back button on the toolbar
   c. choosing the Help menu on the menu bar
   d. clicking the status indicator containing the Netscape corporate logo

STUDENT ASSIGNMENT 3
Understanding the Netscape Window

Instructions: In Figure SA1-3, arrows point to major components of the Netscape window. Identify the various parts of the window in the spaces provided.

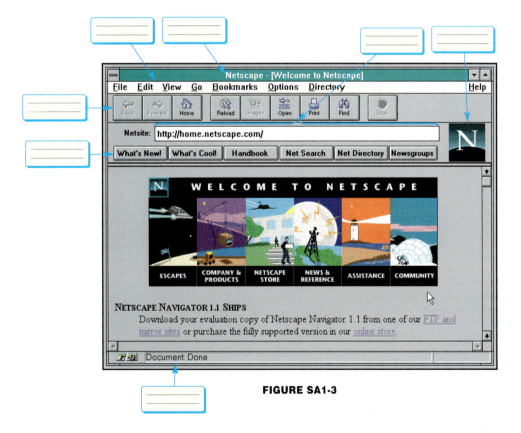

FIGURE SA1-3

STUDENT ASSIGNMENT 4
Understanding Toolbar Buttons

Instructions: In Figure SA1-4, arrows point to several buttons on the Netscape toolbar. In the spaces provided, briefly explain the purpose of each button.

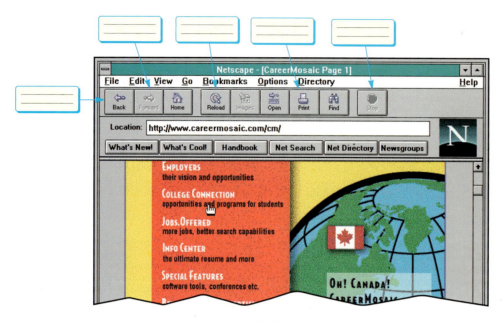

FIGURE SA1-4

STUDENT ASSIGNMENT 5
Understanding Directory Buttons

Instructions: In Figure SA1-5, arrows point to several directory buttons in the Netscape window. In the spaces provided, briefly explain the purpose of each button.

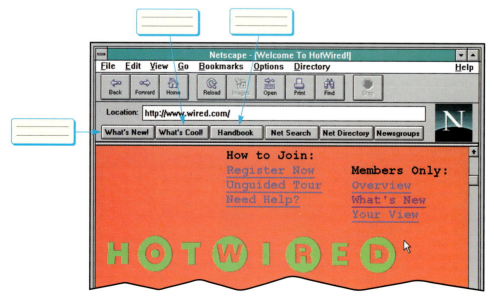

FIGURE SA1-5

STUDENT ASSIGNMENT 6
Understanding Bookmarks

Instructions: Using the Netscape window in Figure SA1-6, list the steps to create a bookmark for the Superconducting Super Collider Laboratory page.

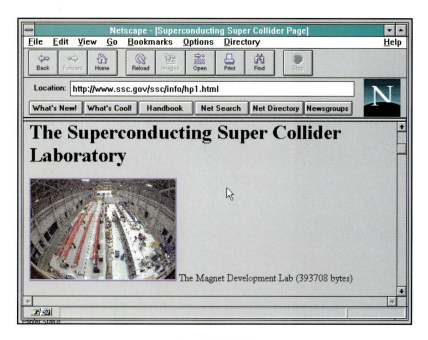

FIGURE SA1-6

1. _____
2. _____
3. _____

H A N D S - O N   E X E R C I S E S

HANDS-ON EXERCISE 1
Using Netscape Help

Purpose: To understand how to obtain help in Netscape.

Instructions: Start Netscape and perform the following tasks with a computer.

1. Click the Handbook directory button.
2. Scroll down to the alphabetical index at the bottom of the page.
3. Using the index, find and display information about bookmarks, as shown in Figure HOE1-1 on the next page.

(continued)

HANDS–ON EXERCISE 1 (continued)

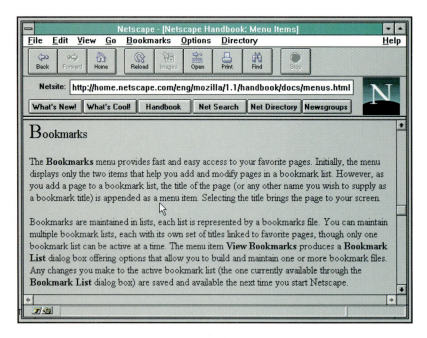

FIGURE HOE1-1

4. Return to the alphabetical index using the Back button on the toolbar.
5. Using the index, find and display information about the Internet.
6. Print the information on the Internet and turn it in to your instructor.

HANDS-ON EXERCISE 2
Printing a Graphical Image

Purpose: To understand how to print pictures displayed with Netscape.

Instructions: Start Netscape and perform the following tasks with a computer.

1. Replace the URL in the URL window with http://www.si.edu/organiza/mallmap.htm and retrieve the page shown in Figure HOE1-2. This will contact the Smithsonian Institute.

2. The words in the picture are links to the corresponding Smithsonian Institute museums. Select one of the museums.

3. Visit the museum.

4. While in the museum, find an interesting picture and display it in the Netscape window.

5. Print the picture on an available printer.

6. Write the URL on the picture and turn it in to your instructor.

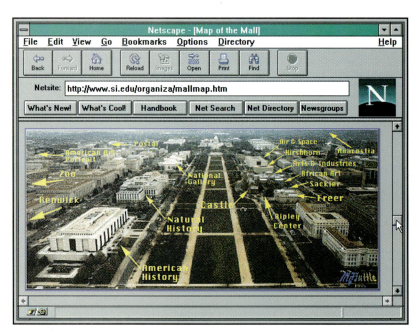

FIGURE HOE1-2

HANDS-ON EXERCISE 3
Saving a Web Page on a Diskette

Purpose: To understand how to save Web pages displayed with Netscape.

Instructions: Start Netscape and perform the following tasks with a computer.

1. Replace the URL in the URL window with http:// owl.trc.purdue.edu/ and retrieve the page shown in Figure HOE1-3. This will contact the English writing lab at Purdue University.
2. Scroll down the page until the link indicating a summary of available topics displays. Select the link.
3. Find and display information about dangling modifiers.
4. Save the Web page to a diskette in drive A.
5. Print the Web page and turn it in to your instructor.

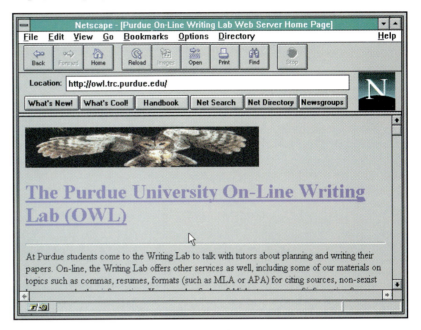

FIGURE HOE1-3

HANDS-ON EXERCISE 4
Managing Bookmarks

Purpose: To understand how to create, use, and remove bookmarks.

Instructions: Start Netscape and perform the following tasks with a computer.

1. Click the What's New button to retrieve the What's New Web page, as shown in Figure HOE1-4.
2. Scroll down the Web page and browse through some of the links found there.
3. When you find a Web page that interests you, add the URL to the bookmark list.
4. Retrieve the Web page again using the bookmark.
5. Remove the bookmark.
6. Verify the bookmark is deleted.

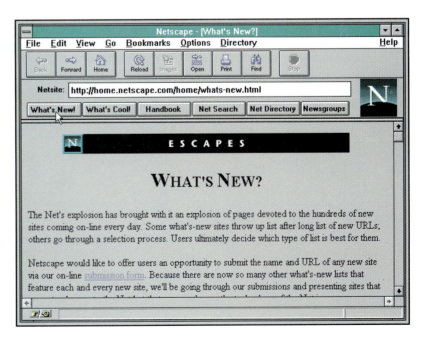

FIGURE HOE1-4

HANDS-ON EXERCISE 5
Printing a Web Page and Using the Clipboard

Purpose: To understand how to print Web pages while in Netscape and use the Clipboard to copy text to other Windows applications.

Instructions: Start Netscape and perform the following tasks with a computer.

1. Replace the URL in the URL window with http://www.whitehouse.gov/ and retrieve the page shown in Figure HOE1-5. This will contact the White House.
2. Select the Publications link.
3. Under National documents, find and print the list of names of the signers of the U.S. Constitution.
4. Copy several names to the Clipboard and then insert the Clipboard contents into Windows Notepad.
5. Save the Notepad file to a diskette in drive A.
6. Print the Notepad file and turn it in to your instructor.

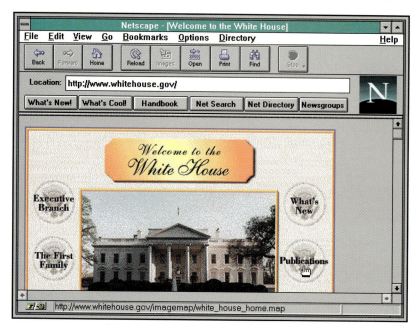

FIGURE HOE1-5

HANDS-ON EXERCISE 6
Saving a Graphical Image on a Diskette

Purpose: To understand how to save pictures displayed with Netscape.

Instructions: Start Netscape and perform the following tasks with a computer.

1. Replace the URL in the URL window with http://clunix.cl.msu.edu/. This will contact Michigan State University.
2. Scroll down the page until the link titled other useful links appears. Select the link.
3. Select current weather maps and movies.
4. Save the current radar/infrared image of the United States weather (Figure HOE1-6) on a diskette in drive A.
5. Print the image and turn it in to your instructor.

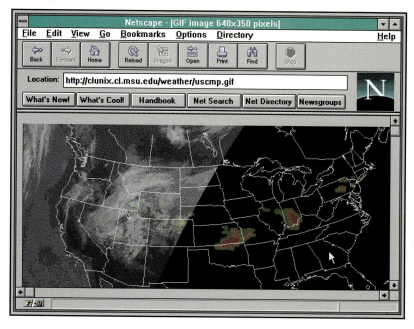

FIGURE HOE1-6

HANDS-ON EXERCISE 7
Sending Information Using Forms

Purposes: To understand how to use interactive forms to send information from Netscape to other Web sites on the Internet.

Instructions: Start Netscape and perform the following tasks with a computer.

1. Replace the URL in the URL window with http://www.irsociety.com/webchat.html. This will contact the Internet Roundtable Society.
2. Scroll down the page until the white WebChat button appears. Click the WebChat button.
3. Click the Click here to enter WebChat button.
4. Scroll down until the chat form displays, as shown in Figure HOE1-7.
5. Enter a handle to identify yourself.
6. Engage someone in conversation. Find out from what part of the world they are participating.
6. Print the Web page containing some of your comments and turn it in to your instructor.

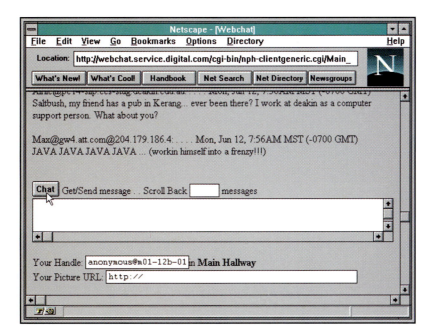

FIGURE HOE1-7

NETSCAPE NAVIGATOR

SEARCHING, RETRIEVING, AND CONVERSING USING NETSCAPE

OBJECTIVES You will have mastered the material in this project when you can:

- Search the Web using InfoSeek
- Search the Web using WebCrawler
- Search the Web using the Internet Directory
- Retrieve files using FTP
- Retrieve files using gopher

- Send and read news group articles
- Perform news group management functions
- Send and receive electronic mail messages
- Perform electronic mail management functions using Eudora

▶ INTRODUCTION

The World Wide Web is growing rapidly every day. The problems of finding the information you seek, usually associated with using the original Internet service programs, are starting to surface with the Web as well. In Project 2, you will learn how to use searching tools created specifically for use on the World Wide Web. In addition, access to traditional non-Web searching and file transfer tools will be shown. Finally two techniques for conversing over the Internet will be covered: news groups and electronic mail.

▶ WEB SEARCH ENGINES

One of the difficult problems with the Internet before the creation of the World Wide Web was finding the files and information in which you were interested. Some primitive Internet search tools such as archie, gopher, and WAIS were developed to address the problem, but even with these tools, you had to learn a command language to use them. Still, using these tools was better than connecting to computer after computer on the Internet, and fruitlessly searching disk directory after disk directory.

Several **search tools** have been developed for searching the World Wide Web. These tools, also called **search engines**, allow you to search the Web in terms of *what* you want, instead of *where* it is located. Most of the search tools are made available as Web pages with a form in which you type **keywords** (a word or phrase) representing topics of items to search for.

Different search tools on the Web perform different types of searches. Some require keywords in the title of Web pages. Others scan hypertext links for the keywords. Still others search the entire text of Web pages. Because of the different searching techniques, the results of the search can sometimes be surprising.

The developers of Netscape realized the need for a searching mechanism, and created a Web page containing access to several of the more popular tools. The following sections show how to start Netscape and access Web searching tools.

Starting Netscape

To start Netscape, follow the steps you used at the beginning of Project 1. These steps are summarized below.

TO START NETSCAPE

Step 1: With Program manager active, open the Netscape group window.
Step 2: Double-click the Netscape program-item icon.

The Netscape window with the Netscape home page displays (Figure 2-1 below).

Accessing the Web Search Tools Page

Because searching is a frequent method of finding information on the Web, Netscape made accessing the Web search tools page easy, as shown in the following steps.

TO ACCESS WEB SEARCH TOOLS ▼

STEP 1 ▶

Point to the Net Search directory button ( ) (Figure 2-1).

The Netscape home page may display differently on your computer because of continuous changes and updates.

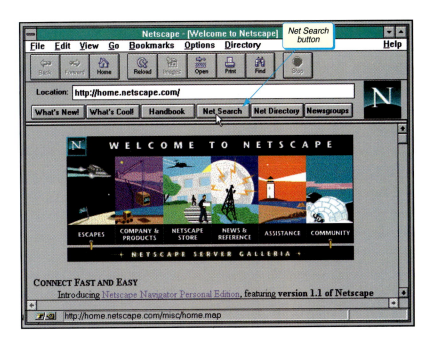

FIGURE 2-1

STEP 2 ▶

Click the Net Search directory button.

The Internet Search page displays (Figure 2-2). The URL of the Internet Search page displays in the URL window. The Internet Search page contains links to several Web search tools found further down on the page.

FIGURE 2-2

STEP 3 ▶

Using the scroll bar on the right side of the screen, scroll down the page.

The InfoSeek input form displays as the first search engine (Figure 2-3). The link to instructions on performing advanced searches displays.

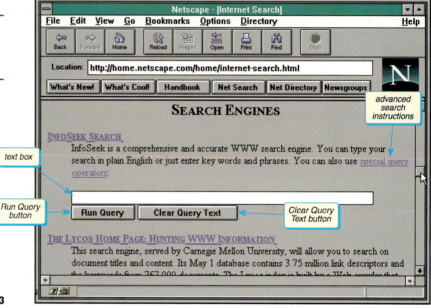

FIGURE 2-3

This form is similar to the form you used in Project 1 to enter comments for WebChat. The form contains a text box where you type the keywords for which to search, a button to run the query or search, and a button to clear the query text box.

Searching the Web Using InfoSeek

InfoSeek is a Web search program made available from InfoSeek Corporation in Santa Clara, California. InfoSeek searches a database of computerized periodicals and more than 400,000 Web pages.

To illustrate using InfoSeek, assume you are writing an informational speech for a speech class, and your topic is the mineral, gold. The following steps show how to use InfoSeek to search for the keyword gold and obtain information about the mineral.

TO PERFORM A WEB SEARCH USING INFOSEEK ▼

STEP 1 ▶

Point to the text box and click the left mouse button. Type `gold` and point to the Run Query button (Run Query) (Figure 2-4).

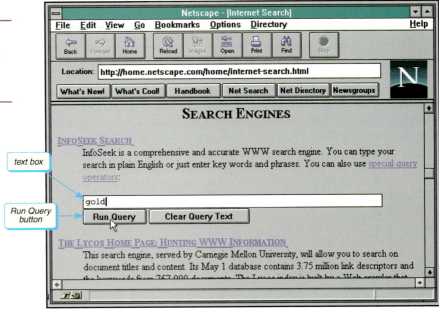

FIGURE 2-4

STEP 2 ▶

Click the Run Query button.

After a brief period of time, the InfoSeek Search Results page displays (Figure 2-5). The page contains a link to new InfoSeek features. Next, the results section identifies the word or phrase used in the search.

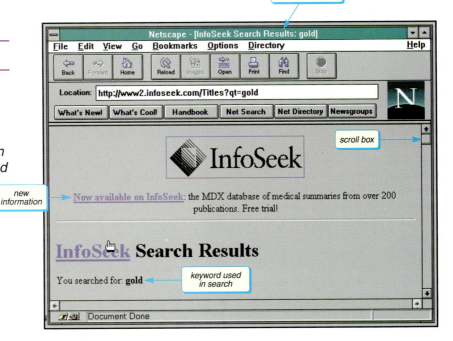

FIGURE 2-5

STEP 3 ▶

Using the scroll box on the right side of the screen, scroll down the page.

Links to Web pages containing the word gold display (Figure 2-6). Along with the links are the first few lines of text from, and the URL of, each Web page.

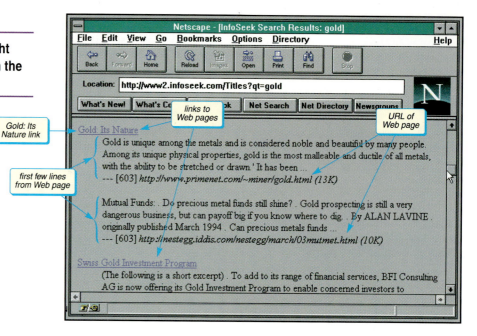

FIGURE 2-6

STEP 4 ▶

Click the Gold: Its Nature link on the first line of the page.

The Web page titled gold.html displays (Figure 2-7). This page is located at a computer provided by Primenet, which is an Internet provider in Phoenix, Arizona.

FIGURE 2-7

STEP 5 ▶

Using the scroll bar, scroll down the page until the Facts about Gold link displays (Figure 2-8).

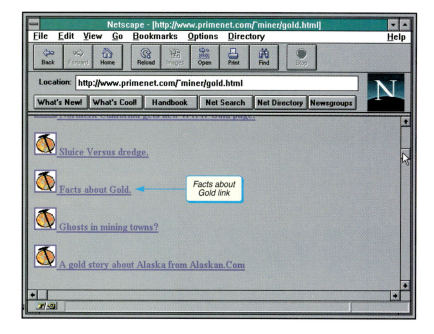

FIGURE 2-8

STEP 6 ▶

Click the Facts about Gold link.

Interesting facts about gold display (Figure 2-9).

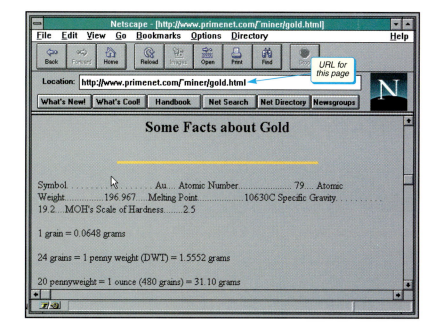

FIGURE 2-9

You can see how easy it is to find information about specific topics, such as the mineral, gold, using InfoSeek and following a few hypertext links. The page containing the information about gold can now be printed or saved on a diskette for use when preparing the informational speech. See the sections in Project 1 on page N22 for saving and page N32 for printing.

You can redisplay the Search results page by clicking the Back button and selecting another link if the first link did not provide the desired results. Or, you can redisplay the Internet Search page to use one of the other search tools.

Redisplaying the Internet Search Page

You can return to the Internet Search page to perform another search or choose another search tool by using the Back button on the toolbar, or by using the history list on the Go menu, as shown in the following steps.

TO REDISPLAY THE INTERNET SEARCH PAGE USING THE HISTORY LIST ▼

STEP 1 ▶

Select the Go menu.

The Go menu displays (Figure 2-10). Notice the history list containing the titles of the pages you have visited. Entry number 3 is the title Internet Search.

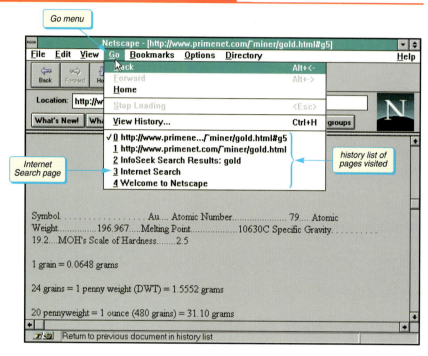

FIGURE 2-10

STEP 2 ▶

Choose Internet Search in the history list.

The Internet Search page redisplays (Figure 2-11).

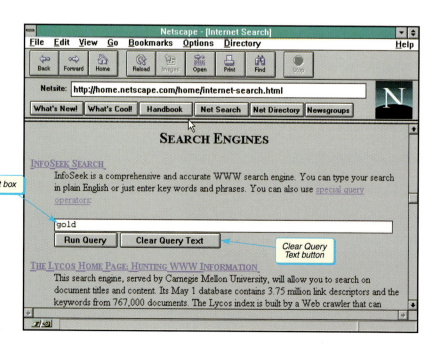

FIGURE 2-11

You can enter other words and phrases for which to search in the text box by dragging the mouse pointer over gold, typing another word or phrase, and clicking the Run Query button. You can also start a new search by clicking the Clear Query button, typing a new word or phrase in the text box, and clicking the Run Query button.

Searching the Web Using WebCrawler

Another World Wide Web search tool available from the Internet Search page is called WebCrawler. **WebCrawler** is a Web search program administered by America Online. WebCrawler uses a program that travels around the World Wide Web looking for topics, automatically following links it finds, and adding them to a searchable index.

To illustrate using WebCrawler, assume you are assembling information about different mutual funds and want to know the historic equity performance for the Twentieth Century family of mutual funds. Twentieth Century Mutual Funds, from Kansas City, Missouri, provides several popular mutual funds for retirement plans, as well as individual investors. To start the search, display the WebCrawler search page, as shown in the following steps.

TO DISPLAY THE WEBCRAWLER PAGE ▼

STEP 1 ▶

If necessary, click the Net Search directory button to display the Internet Search page. Scroll down the Internet Search page until the WebCrawler Searching link displays (Figure 2-12).

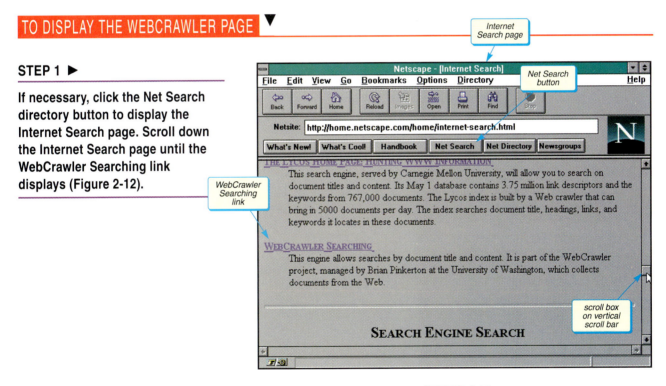

FIGURE 2-12

STEP 2 ▶

Click the WebCrawler Searching link.

The WebCrawler Searching page displays (Figure 2-13). This page displays instructions for entering keywords and a button to initiate the search. The Number of results to return box indicates how many URLs of pages containing the keywords should be returned.

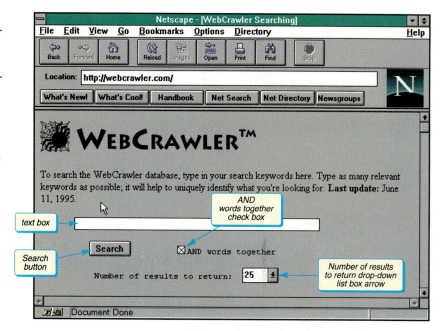

FIGURE 2-13

Like InfoSeek, WebCrawler has a text box where you enter keywords and a Search button to start the search. The AND words together check box indicates whether keywords you enter, separated by a space, should both appear together in a Web page to be considered a match. Notice the Number of results to return drop-down list box where you can control how many URLs of Web pages containing your keywords to return. The default is 25. You can adjust the number of results returned, as shown in the following steps.

TO ADJUST THE NUMBER OF RESULTS RETURNED BY WEBCRAWLER ▼

STEP 1 ▶

Click the Number of results to return drop-down list box arrow.

A drop-down list box displays a list of suggested numbers (Figure 2-14).

STEP 2 ▶

Click 100 in the drop-down list.

The box disappears, and the number 100 displays in the Number of results to return drop-down list box.

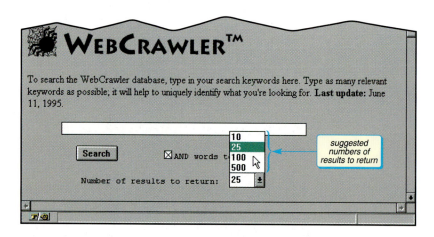

FIGURE 2-14

Some searches can return thousands of URLs, so limiting the number to return can reduce the amount of links you have to look through. You must select one of the numbers in the box. Having set the number of URLs to return, you can now perform the search. Because you are interested in mutual funds, the words, *mutual funds*, is a good phrase to use as keywords for this search.

TO PERFORM A WEB SEARCH USING WEBCRAWLER ▼

STEP 1 ▶

Click the text box. Type `mutual funds` (Figure 2-15). Point to the Search button.

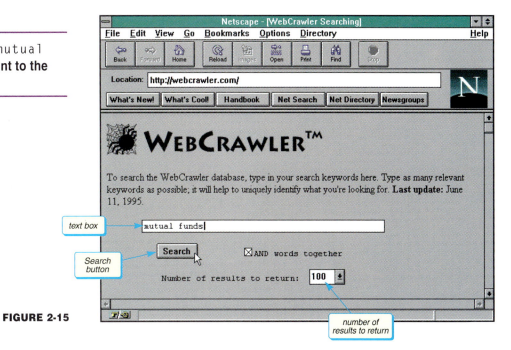

FIGURE 2-15

STEP 2 ▶

Click the Search button.

After a brief period of time, the WebCrawler Search Results page displays (Figure 2-16). The time required for the search will depend on the number selected in the Number of results to return drop-down list box. On the WebCrawler Search Results page, the number that appears on the left side of each link reflects the relevance of the page to your keywords, with a score of 500 being half as relevant as a perfect score of 1000.

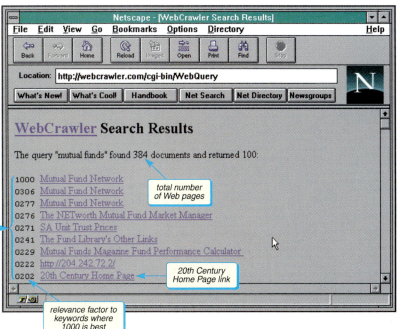

FIGURE 2-16

STEP 3 ▶

Click the 20th Century Home Page link.

The 20th Century Home Page displays (Figure 2-17). The URL for 20th Century Home Page displays in the URL window.

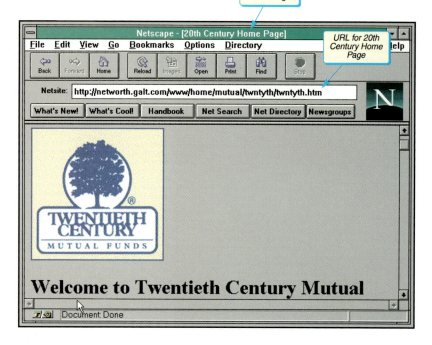

FIGURE 2-17

STEP 4 ▶

Scroll down the page until the Twentieth Century's Equity Performance link displays (Figure 2-18). Point to the Twentieth Century's Equity Performance link.

Notice the links to other information provided by 20th Century, such as retirement data and descriptions of its mutual funds.

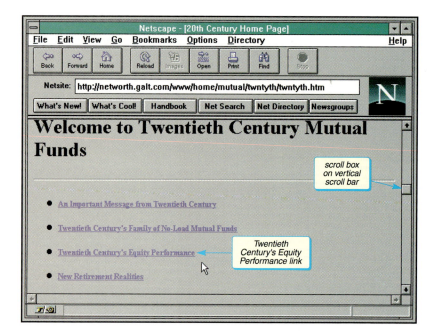

FIGURE 2-18

STEP 5 ▶

Click the Twentieth Century's Equity Performance link.

The Equity Performance page displays (Figure 2-19).The URL for the Equity Performance page displays in the URL window. Equity Performance figures are further down the page.

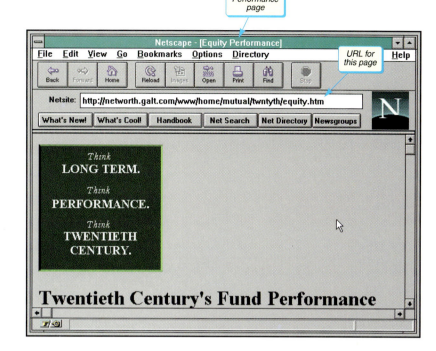

FIGURE 2-19

STEP 6 ▶

Scroll down the page to reveal the performance figures (Figure 2-20).

Each line represents one mutual fund with the name of the fund on the left. The columns represent the yearly increases of your investment if you left your money in a particular fund for 1 year, 5 years, 10 years, 20 years, or for the life of the fund.

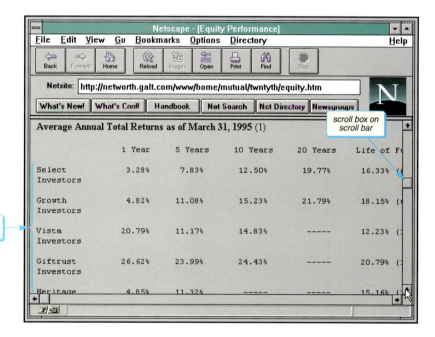

FIGURE 2-20

The equity performance results shown in Figure 2-20 are the same as those sent out through the mail if you called Twentieth Century and requested a prospectus. If you scroll down the page, you can read additional information about the funds and request more information and a prospectus from this mutual fund company.

Searching the Web Using the Yahoo Directory

Another valuable Web search engine uses a series of menus to organize links to Web pages without requiring you to enter keywords. Starting with general categories and getting increasingly more specific as links are selected, the **Yahoo Directory** provides a menu-like interface for searching the Web.

To illustrate using the Yahoo Directory, assume you are taking an anatomy course and want to search the World Wide Web for information about the human heart. To begin the search, display the Yahoo Directory Web page, as shown in the following steps.

TO DISPLAY THE YAHOO DIRECTORY WEB PAGE ▼

STEP 1 ▶

Point to the Net Directory button on the toolbar and click.

The Internet Directory page displays (Figure 2-21). Information about the Yahoo Directory is shown. The actual directory is further down the page.

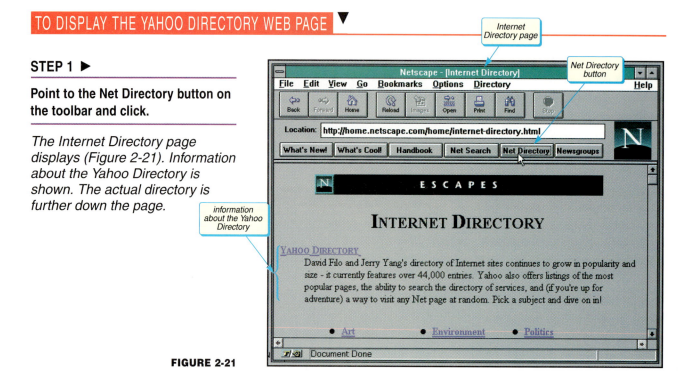

FIGURE 2-21

STEP 2 ▶

Scroll down the page to reveal the top-level Yahoo Directory list.

The directory is organized into broad categories (Figure 2-22). Each category is a link to a Web page containing more detailed topics about the broader category.

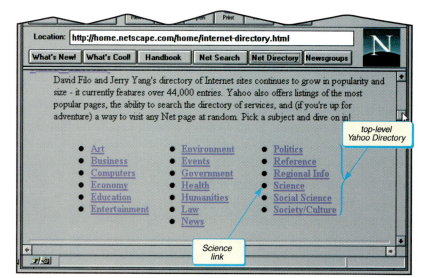

FIGURE 2-22

Web pages in the Yahoo Directory are organized into the broad categories you see in Figure 2-22. You have to decide into which category your search topic falls, and select the corresponding link. When you select the link, another page of links displays with more specific topics from which to choose. You continue following the links until you find the information you are looking for. The following steps show how to navigate through the Yahoo Directory to retrieve information about the human heart.

TO PERFORM A WEB SEARCH USING THE YAHOO DIRECTORY ▼

STEP 1 ►

Click the Science link.

The Yahoo Science page displays (Figure 2-23). Notice the links represent different areas of science. The number next to the link indicates how many Web pages you will find if you click that link. The word [new] to the right of a link indicates the link has been updated recently. Because biology is the branch of science that deals with living things, the Biology link is likely to have information about the human heart.

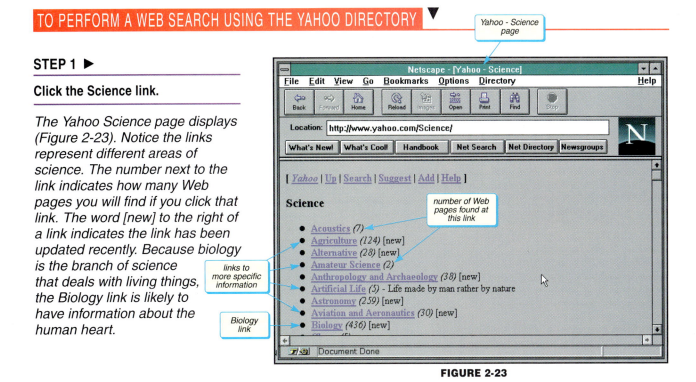

FIGURE 2-23

STEP 2 ►

Click the Biology link.

The Yahoo Science:Biology page displays (Figure 2-24). These links represent different areas of biology. Because the heart is part of the human anatomy, the Anatomy link is likely to have information about the human heart.

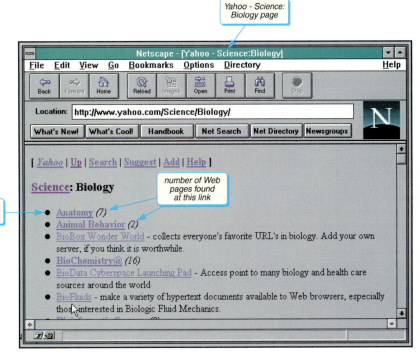

FIGURE 2-24

STEP 3 ▶

Click the Anatomy link.

The Yahoo - Science:Biology: Anatomy page displays (Figure 2-25). The second link, Institute, contains links to two Web pages, making the total number of pages available from this page, 7. The third link holds information about the human heart.

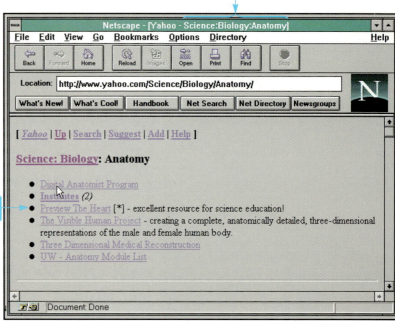

FIGURE 2-25

STEP 4 ▶

Click the Preview The Heart link. Point to the eyeball at the bottom of the screen.

*The Preview the Heart page displays (Figure 2-26). The picture in the display area is a selectable map. A **selectable map** is a picture that has different URLs associated with different areas of the picture. You can display a different Web page depending on where the mouse pointer is located in the map when you click the mouse button.*

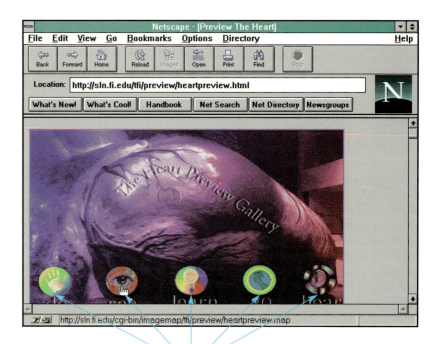

FIGURE 2-26

STEP 5 ▶

Click the left mouse button.

The Heart: Things To See page displays (Figure 2-27). Entering the URL in the URL window will also cause the Web page to display. A link to a picture of a human heart is further down the page.

FIGURE 2-27

STEP 6 ▶

Scroll down the page. Click the Development of The Heart link.

The Development of the Human Heart page displays (Figure 2-28). Scrolling down the page, you will find information about the development of the human heart and a link to the picture of the heart.

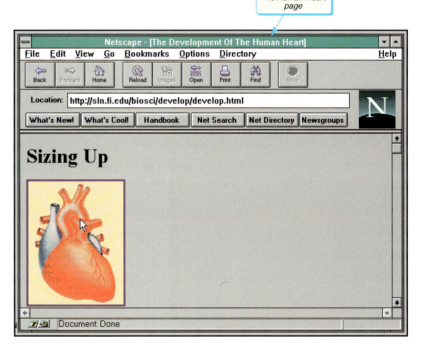

FIGURE 2-28

STEP 7 ▶

Scroll down the page. Click the link **View the structure of a preserved human heart.**

A picture of an actual, preserved human heart displays (Figure 2-29).

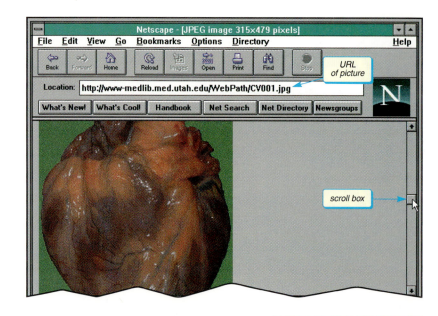

FIGURE 2-29

The picture of the heart can now be printed or saved to a disk file and used in your anatomy class, as an illustration in a report, for example. See the sections in Project 1 on page N22 for saving, and page N32 for printing.

Redisplaying the Yahoo Directory

You can redisplay the top-level Yahoo Directory using the history list on the Go menu, just like you used it to redisplay the Internet Search page, as shown in the following steps.

TO REDISPLAY THE YAHOO DIRECTORY PAGE USING THE HISTORY LIST ▼

STEP 1 ▶

Select the Go menu.

The Go menu displays (Figure 2-30). Notice the history list of pages you have visited.

STEP 2 ▶

Choose Internet Directory in the history list.

The Internet Directory page redisplays, as shown previously in Figure 2-21 on page N68.

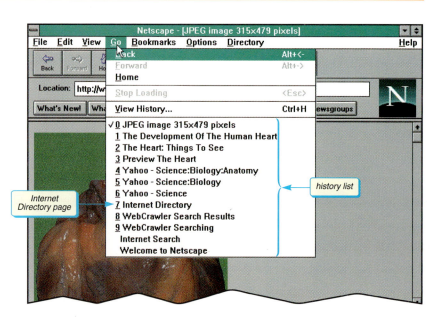

FIGURE 2-30

You have learned how to search the World Wide Web using three of the most popular Web search engines: InfoSeek, WebCrawler and the Yahoo Directory. Table 2-1 summarizes these search engines and the search methods used.

The search tools discussed in Table 2-1 are the three most popular on the Web. Many other Web searching engines are available.

Although searching engines such as those in Table 2-1 help you sort through the millions of Web pages available on the World Wide Web, many more files and programs are available on the Internet that are not part of the World Wide Web. The following section introduces you to a way to access these files and programs using a program called FTP.

▶ **TABLE 2-1**

SEARCH ENGINE	SEARCH METHOD
InfoSeek	Searches database of computerized periodicals and more than 400,000 Web pages; database maintained by InfoSeek Corporation
WebCrawler	Searches index of Web pages; program travels around Web finding pages
Yahoo Directory	Traverses topic-based menus; pages submitted by authors for inclusion in menus

▶ RETRIEVING FILES WITH FTP

The second most popular activity on the Internet, after electronic mail, is transferring files. With FTP, you can retrieve software, data files, word processing documents, graphics, pictures, movies and sound clips.

The program that assists in this is called **FTP**, or **File Transfer Protocol**. This program moves files between different computer systems. The FTP program has a set of commands that are used to transfer files and perform file management tasks. When using FTP within Netscape, however, no commands are necessary. You use the point and click method, similar to following hypertext links.

Unfortunately, you have to know the URL of the computer where these files are located. Using the many well-known FTP sites, called **repositories**, or **FTP archives**, you can access a variety of interesting programs and files stored for public access. As you gain experience with the Internet, you will discover more FTP sites for which you can create bookmarks. See page N17 in Project 1 for information on creating bookmarks.

To illustrate using FTP in Netscape, you will connect to ftp.cdrom.com, a popular FTP site, and transfer a program called Eudora, a Windows-based electronic mail program. The following steps show how to establish an FTP session in Netscape.

TO CONNECT TO FTP.CDROM.COM USING FTP ▼

STEP 1

Drag the mouse pointer over the entire URL in the URL window.

The URL is highlighted (Figure 2-31).

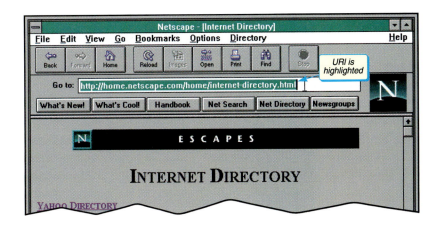

FIGURE 2-31

STEP 2 ▶

Type ftp://ftp.cdrom.com
(Figure 2-32).

FIGURE 2-32

STEP 3 ▶

Press the ENTER key.

The current directory page displays (Figure 2-33). The name of the current directory is shown, followed by information about the FTP site. Links to files and directories available at the FTP site are located at the bottom of the page.

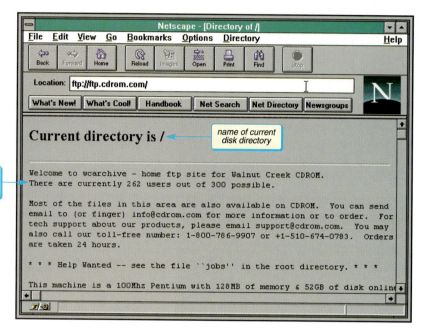

FIGURE 2-33

STEP 4 ▶

Scroll down until the scroll box is at the bottom of the scroll bar.

The bottom of the current directory page displays (Figure 2-34). The icons on the left represent different types of files. The names of the files display next to the icons.

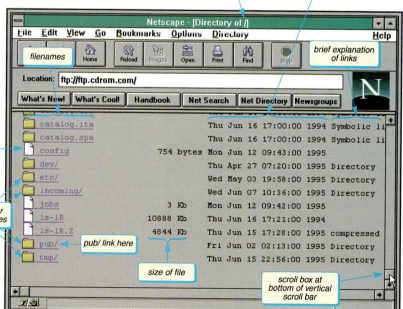

FIGURE 2-34

When connecting to an FTP site using Netscape, the page in the display area will contain a listing of all the files and directories that are stored in the current directory. Most FTP sites are divided into directories, providing smaller, more manageable lists of files than if all the files on the disk displayed in one long list.

You can move around within the directory structure by clicking directory links in the current directory page. The **current directory** is the disk directory in the site's directory structure. The current directory is displayed in the title bar of the Netscape window. The slash in the title bar in Figure 2-34 indicates the root directory of the FTP site.

Notice in Figure 2-34 the pictures, or icons, next to the filenames. Each icon represents a different type of file and lets you know what will happen when that link is clicked. Table 2-2 summarizes the icons and their meanings.

▶ **TABLE 2-2**

ICON	REPRESENTS	ACTION TAKEN
📁	directory	Moves to a new subdirectory
📄	document	Transfers a text file to your computer
📄	file	Transfers an unknown type of file to your computer
📄	executable program	Transfers a ready-to-execute file to your computer

Navigating through Public Access FTP Directories

Most FTP sites organize their files into directories using some logical technique such as by computer operating system, such as MSDOS, or UNIX, or by general software topic, such as graphics, or utilities. The starting directory for public access is traditionally called **pub**, which is the second link from the bottom in Figure 2-34. The search for Eudora starts there. The following steps show how to navigate through the public access FTP directories.

TO NAVIGATE THROUGH PUBLIC ACCESS FTP DIRECTORIES ▼

STEP 1 ▶

Click the pub/ link, which is the second link from the bottom in Figure 2-34.

The Directory of /pub page displays (Figure 2-35). This directory page contains many categories of software organized into subdirectories.

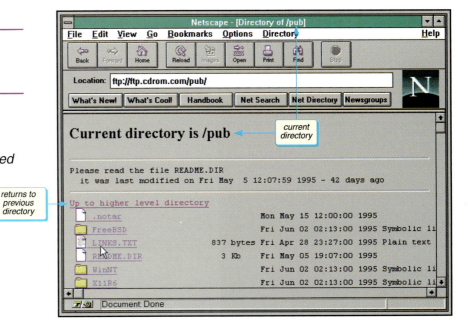

current directory

returns to previous directory

FIGURE 2-35

STEP 2 ▶

Scroll down to the bottom of the page.

Several available directories display (Figure 2-36). One of them is simtel. This directory contains copies of all the publicly available software stored in a repository located at the U.S. Army White Sands Missile Range computer in New Mexico.

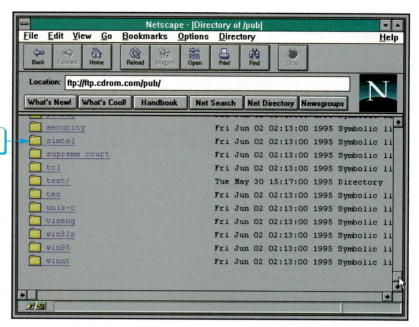

FIGURE 2-36

STEP 3 ▶

Click the simtel link.

The Directory of /pub/simtel page displays (Figure 2-37). The simtel directory contains software organized into directories by operating system name. The directory links are located further down the page.

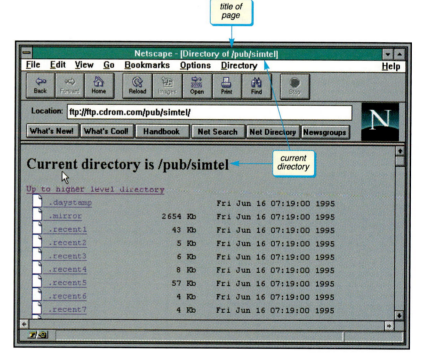

FIGURE 2-37

STEP 4 ▶

Scroll down to the bottom of the page.

Several directories display (Figure 2-38) containing software for different operating systems. The win3/ directory holds software for Windows version 3. Because Eudora runs under Windows, it is likely to be found in the win3/ directory.

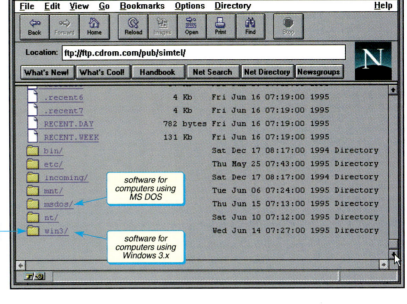

FIGURE 2-38

STEP 5 ▶

Click the win3/ link.

The Directory of /pub/simtel/win3 page displays (Figure 2-39). Notice instructions directing you to read certain files that contain important information about activities such as file transfers and how to upload files.

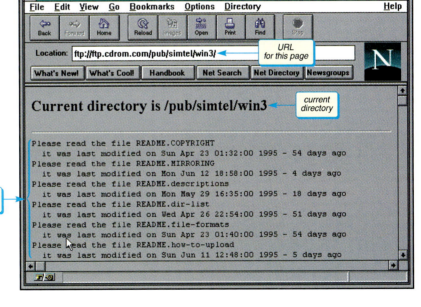

FIGURE 2-39

STEP 6 ▶

Scroll down the page until the eudora/ link displays (Figure 2-40).

Notice that the software in the win3/ directory is now organized by categories; fileutil for file utilities and graphics for computer graphics.

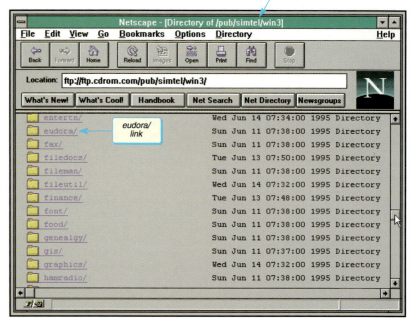

FIGURE 2-40

STEP 7 ▶

Click the eudora/ link.

The Directory of /pub/simtel/win3/eudora page displays (Figure 2-41).

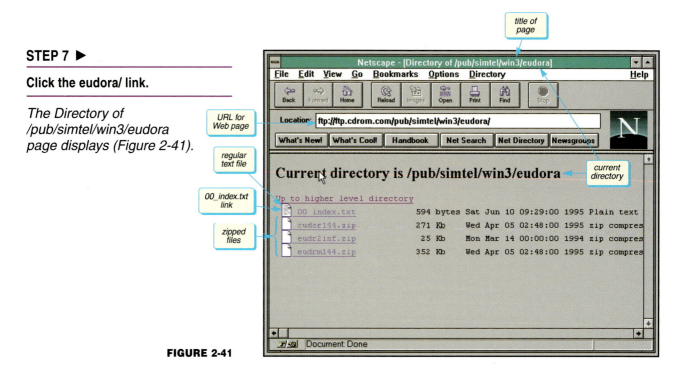

FIGURE 2-41

Notice the four files in the directory. The first, 00_index.txt, is a text file. The other three are files that have been specially processed with a program called zip. The **zip** program combines several files into one file, making it easier to transfer a number of programs and files over the Internet. After you retrieve a zipped file, you have to unzip it before you can use it. Later in the project, you are shown how to obtain an unzip program so you can unzip your copy of Eudora.

Most public access FTP sites have an index for all the files stored in a particular directory. At ftp.cdrom.com, the index files are called 00_index.txt. You can look at the index to see which of the three Eudora files should be retrieved. To see what the index contains you have to retrieve it, as shown in the following steps.

TO RETRIEVE FILES USING FTP ▼

STEP 1 ▶

Insert a formatted diskette in drive A. There should be at lease 313KB of space available on the diskette to carry out these steps.

Back button

STEP 2 ▶

Click the 00_index.txt link.

The contents of the 00_index.txt file displays (Figure 2-42). Descriptions of the three zip files are available. The descriptions indicate that the first file, eudor144.zip, is the one you want.

contains Eudora for Windows program

contains documentation for Eudora

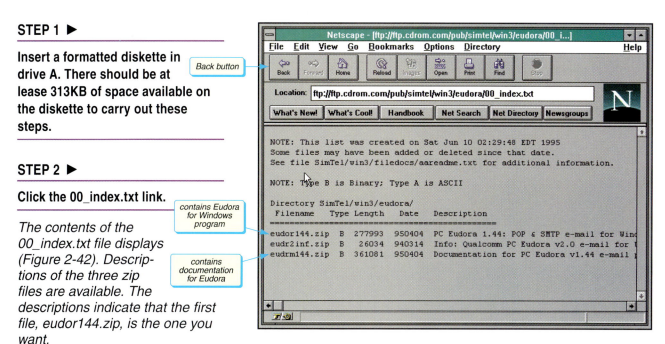

FIGURE 2-42

STEP 3 ▶

Click the Back button on the Netscape toolbar.

Back button

The Directory of /pub/simtel/win3/eudora redisplays (Figure 2-43).

eudor144.zip link

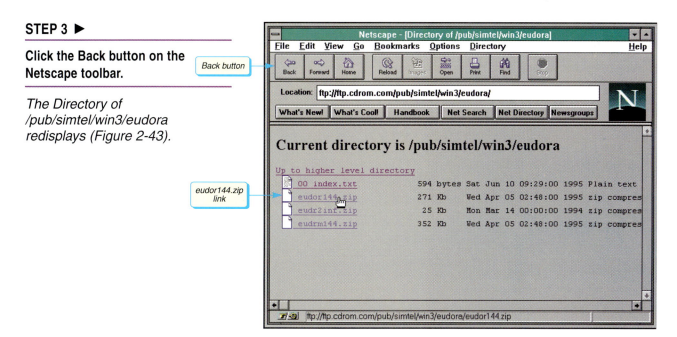

FIGURE 2-43

STEP 4 ▶

Click the eudor144.zip link.

The Unknown File Type dialog box displays (Figure 2-44). The three available actions are cancel the transfer, save the file to disk, or configure a viewer. **Viewers** *are special helper programs that are used to process special file types such as movies and sound clips.*

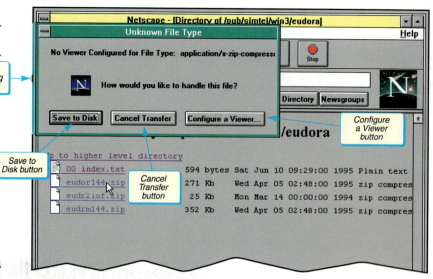

FIGURE 2-44

STEP 5 ▶

Click the Save to Disk button.

A Save as dialog box appears (Figure 2-45) with eudor144.zip as the default file name.

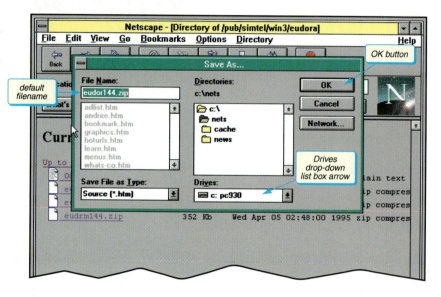

FIGURE 2-45

STEP 6 ▶

Click the Drives drop-down list box arrow and select drive A.

Drive A becomes the current drive (Figure 2-46). If the drive A icon does not display in the Drives drop-down list box, click the scroll bar to bring it into view.

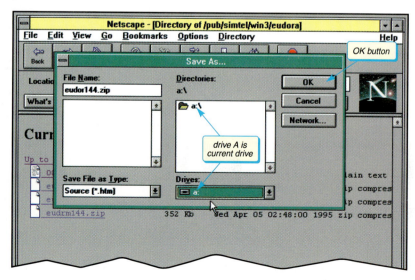

FIGURE 2-46

STEP 7 ▶

Choose the OK button in the Save As dialog box.

The Save As dialog box disappears. The Eudora program is retrieved as shown at the bottom of Figure 2-47 and saved on the diskette in drive A using the filename eudor144.zip.

FIGURE 2-47

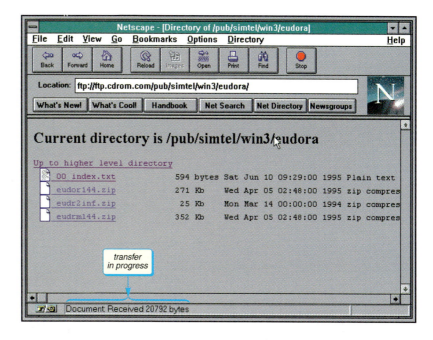

You have successfully retrieved the latest version of the Eudora mail program. You can retrieve the Eudora documentation file (eudrm144.zip) in the same fashion.

Retrieving a Copy of Unzip

The Eudora program is still not usable in its zipped format. You will have to unzip it before you can use it. The following steps retrieve a copy of the unzip program you can use to unzip the Eudora file.

TO OBTAIN A COPY OF UNZIP ▼

STEP 1 ▶

Click the Back button on the toolbar.

The Directory of /pub/simtel/win3 page redisplays, as shown in Figure 2-40 on page N78.

STEP 2 ▶

Scroll up toward the top of the page until the UNZIP.EXE link displays (Figure 2-48).

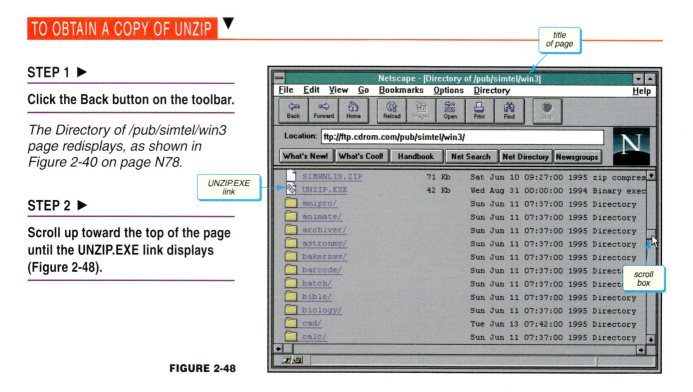

FIGURE 2-48

STEP 3 ▶

Click the UNZIP.EXE link. Click the Save to Disk button in the Unknown File Type dialog box (Figure 2-44 on page N80).

The Save As dialog box displays (Figure 2-49) with unzip.exe as the default filename. Drive A is the current drive.

STEP 4 ▶

Choose the OK button to save unzip.exe on the diskette in drive A.

The Save As dialog box disappears. The file unzip.exe is transferred and saved to drive A.

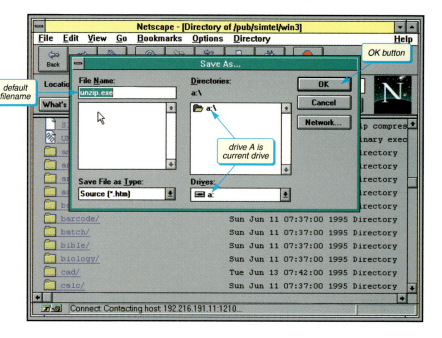

FIGURE 2-49

Now that you have the unzip program, you can use it to unzip Eudora for use with Windows. See Appendix B for instructions on installing Eudora.

You have learned how to retrieve files using FTP. You might want to create a bookmark of this page, so Netscape can bring you right back here when you want to retrieve other Windows software programs. See the section on creating bookmarks in Project 1 on page N17. Thousands of other FTP sites exist to check out. Appendix A contains several popular and useful public access FTP sites.

FTP is one of the service programs that was part of the Internet long before the World Wide Web. Another Internet service program that pre-dates the World Wide Web, but is still very useful, is called gopher

▶ USING GOPHER TO RETRIEVE FILES

Initially developed at the University of Minnesota to help its users find answers to local computing questions, **gopher** has since developed into a worldwide service that helps organize the vast collection of information available on the Internet.

Gopher started out as a document retrieval system. Over time, it has been modified to serve as a user-friendly, menu-driven way of retrieving files. Much like FTP, when using gopher you are presented with a list of menu items. Choosing one of the items might display additional items or retrieve that item and store it on your computer.

You access a gopher site the same way you accessed the FTP site, by supplying a URL that Netscape can use to connect to the gopher site. The following steps show how to connect to the gopher at the University of Michigan in Ann Arbor, Michigan and display 1990 census data on the educational attainment levels of the population of the United States.

TO START A GOPHER SESSION ▼

STEP 1 ▶

Drag the mouse pointer over the URL in the URL window. Type `gopher://una.hh.lib .umich.edu` **(Figure 2-50).**

The FTP URL disappears when the new URL is typed.

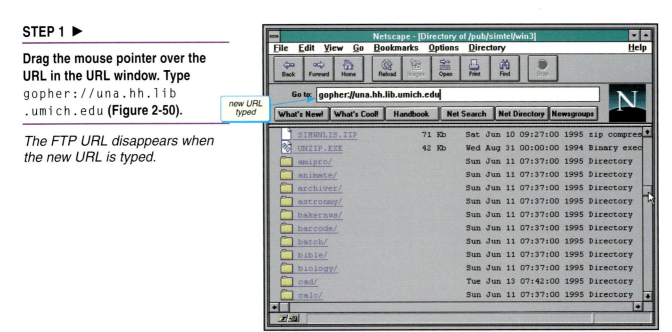

FIGURE 2-50

STEP 2 ▶

Press the ENTER key.

The Gopher Menu page displays (Figure 2-51). The icons and associated links represent lower level gopher menus, each containing several links.

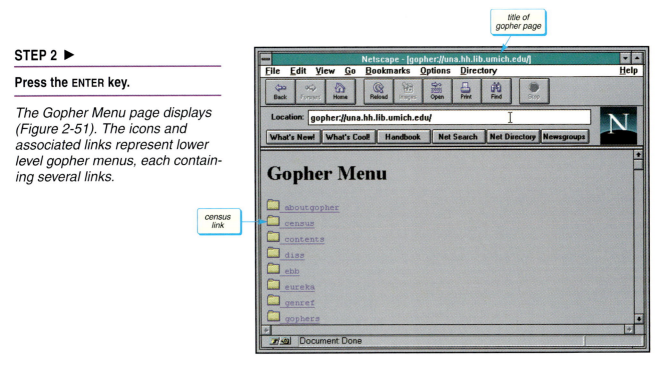

FIGURE 2-51

Navigating Gopher Menus

The layout of the gopher menus is similar to the FTP directory pages discussed earlier. There are links to other menu items that are identified by the same icons used with FTP (see Table 2-2 on page N75). To navigate through the gopher menus to find the census data, click the census link, as shown in the following steps.

TO NAVIGATE GOPHER MENUS ▼

STEP 1 ▶

Click the census link in the column of links under the Gopher Menu (Figure 2-51 on the previous page).

The census page displays (Figure 2-52). This page includes documents describing the census gopher, census data, and other census information. U.S. census data is located further down the page.

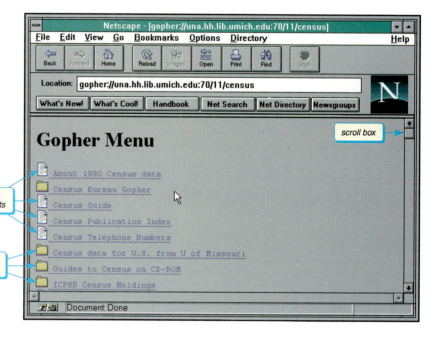

FIGURE 2-52

STEP 2 ▶

Scroll down the page until the United States summaries link displays (Figure 2-53).

U.S. census data can be found through the United States summaries link.

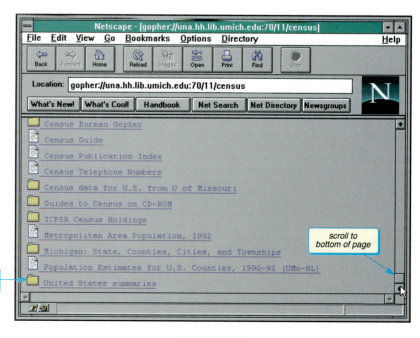

FIGURE 2-53

STEP 3 ►

Click the United States summaries link.

The Gopher Menu summaries page displays (Figure 2-54). Education levels are located under the 1990 U.S. social, economic and housing data link.

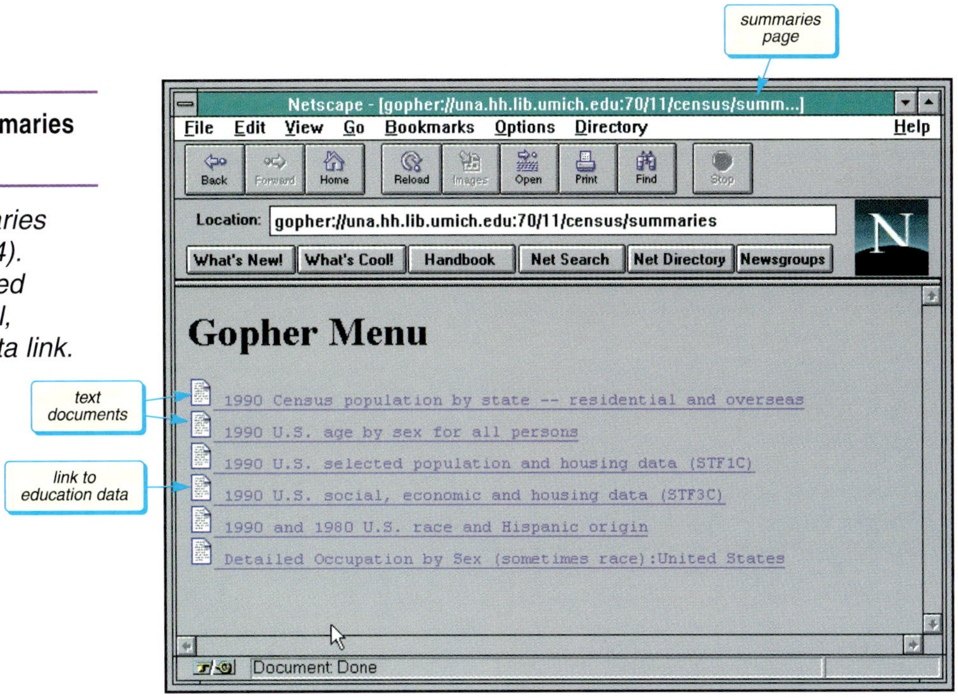

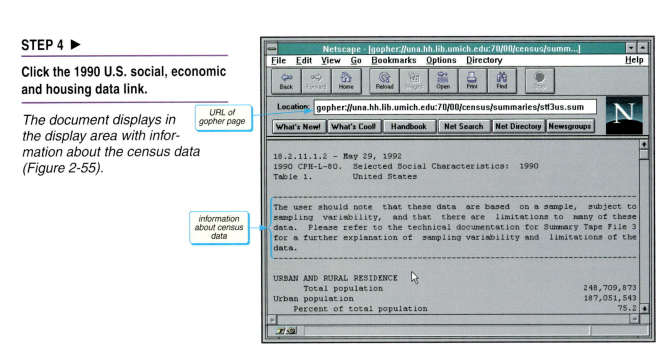

FIGURE 2-54

STEP 4 ►

Click the 1990 U.S. social, economic and housing data link.

The document displays in the display area with information about the census data (Figure 2-55).

FIGURE 2-55

STEP 5 ▶

Scroll down the page to reveal the educational level information (Figure 2-56).

Educational attainment levels as well as other interesting classifications of the U.S. population display.

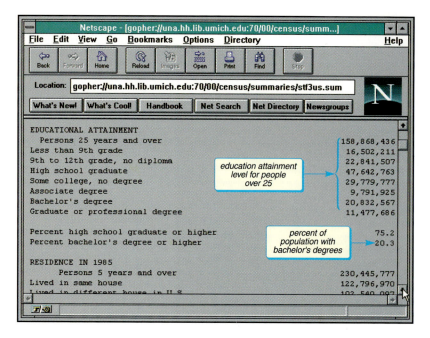

FIGURE 2-56

You can see that 75% of the adult population has at least a high school diploma, and 20% of the population has at least a bachelor's degree. The displayed page can now be printed or saved on a diskette.

If you want to study other U.S. census information, you can move back to the previous gopher menus by clicking the Back button on the Netscape toolbar.

Just as there are many public access FTP sites, there are many public access gopher sites you can contact. See Appendix A for the locations of other interesting gopher sites.

Transferring files over the Internet is only part of the communications capabilities available. Project 2 continues with a discussion of two Internet services that allow people from all over the world with similar interests to get together electronically and share their thoughts and opinions on thousands of topics. The services are news groups and electronic mail.

▶ NEWS GROUPS

I t is human nature for people with similar interests to be drawn together to discuss and share their thoughts, information, opinions, and research. Sometimes, people form clubs or discussion groups where they can talk and exchange ideas about their mutual interests.

A very large number of electronic discussion groups called **news groups** are available on the Internet. Using Netscape, you can **post**, or send, to the news group your thoughts and opinions about a particular topic, and read what other people have to say. The articles that accumulate on a particular topic are called a **thread**. Figure 2-57 shows some articles and threads from a news group called alt.best.of.internet.

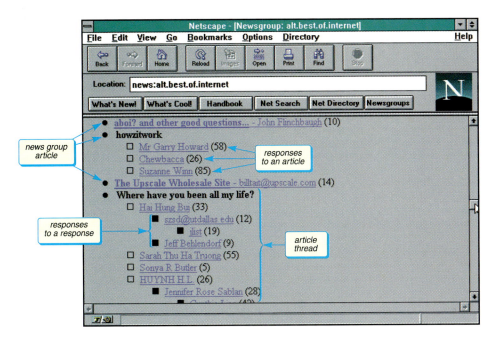

FIGURE 2-57

News groups exist on vendor products such as Novell, Microsoft, IBM, and UNIX, on subjects such as recipes, gardening, and music, or on just about any other topic you can think of. The discussion topics are organized into broad categories, some of which are listed in Table 2-3.

A news group name might begin with one of these category prefixes, followed by one or more words that narrow down the main topic of the group. The news group name comp.lang.pascal is a group interested in computers. The group further limits discussions to programming languages, specifically, Pascal.

These news group prefixes are by no means the only ones used. New news groups are being created everyday.

Accessing USENET with Netscape

USENET is the term used to describe the collection of computer sites that has agreed to share and forward the thousands of discussion groups. The steps on the next page illustrate how you can use Netscape to access USENET news groups.

▶ **TABLE 2-3**

PREFIX	DESCRIPTION
alt	Groups on alternative topics
biz	Business topics
comp	Computer topics
gnu	GNU software foundation topics
ieee	Electrical engineering topics
info	Information about various topics
misc	Miscellaneous topics
news	Groups pertaining to the USENET news
rec	Recreational topics
sci	Science topics
talk	Various discussion groups

TO ACCESS NEWS GROUPS IN NETSCAPE ▼

STEP 1 ▶

Click the Newsgroups directory button.

The News group Server list page displays (Figure 2-58). The page contains a list of available USENET computer sites.

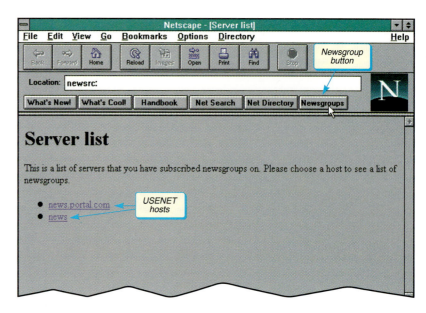

FIGURE 2-58

STEP 2 ▶

Point to news.portal.com and click the left mouse pointer. If news.portal.com does not display in your list, ask your instructor which USENET computer site you should use.

The Subscribed Newsgroups page displays (Figure 2-59). The page contains a description of the contents of the page along with instructions for subscribing and unsubscribing to news groups.

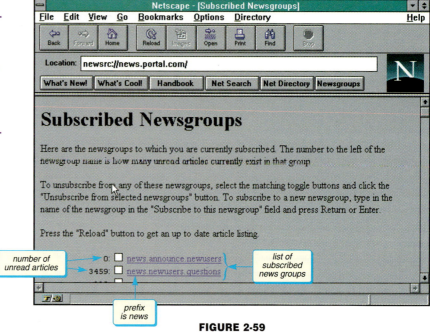

FIGURE 2-59

The Subscribed Newsgroup page contains a list of the news groups to which a user is currently subscribed. **Subcribed** means you have selected these groups as the ones you want to visit most frequently. The news groups you see listed are the default groups everyone is automatically subscribed to when first accessing USENET. The default news groups may be different at your school.

Netscape will keep the names of subscribed news groups in a special file and make them available every time you click the Newsgroups button. You will subscribe to news groups later in the project.

Notice the prefix of the listed news group names is news. This indicates the topic of these groups is USENET and news groups. These are only a few of the thousands of news groups available. The following steps show how to display a list of all the available news groups

TO DISPLAY ALL AVAILABLE NEWS GROUPS ▼

STEP 1 ▶

Scroll down to the bottom of the Subscribed Newsgroups page to bring the View all newsgroups button (View all newsgroups) into view (Figure 2-60).

The View all newsgroups button causes a list of all available news group names to display.

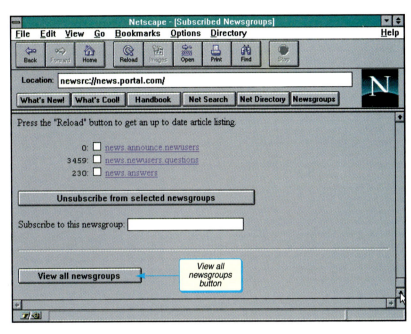

FIGURE 2-60

STEP 2 ▶

Click the View all newsgroups button.

A Netscape dialog box displays, indicating the transfer could take a long time (Figure 2-61). Remember, thousands of news groups exist. Notice the message says you can open another Netscape window and continue browsing the Web while the list of news group names is retrieved.

FIGURE 2-61

STEP 3 ▶

Click the OK button in the Netscape dialog box.

The Newsgroups list page displays (Figure 2-62). The page contains links to news groups and to collections of news groups that all start with a common prefix.

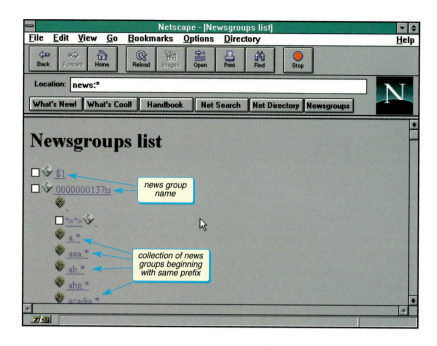

FIGURE 2-62

The list contains two types of entries. The first, identified by the white box on the same line, are news groups you can enter to read articles. The second type of entry, without a white box, represents a collection of news groups that all begin with the letters you see before the asterisk (*). Clicking one of these links displays a page with links to news groups that all start with that specific prefix. This makes the list of all news groups somewhat shorter and easier to scan.

Selecting a News Group

With the list of available news groups displayed, you can select one and descend into it to read the articles there. To illustrate how to select a news group, the following steps show how to display the biz.jobs.offered news group to see what kinds of jobs are available in the business world. Recall that news groups that begin with biz are business-related. See Table 2-3 on page N87.

TO DISPLAY THE BIZ.JOBS.OFFERED NEWS GROUP ▼

STEP 1 ▶

Scroll down the page until the biz.* link appears in the display window (Figure 2-63).

The biz. link links to a page containing news groups that start with biz.*

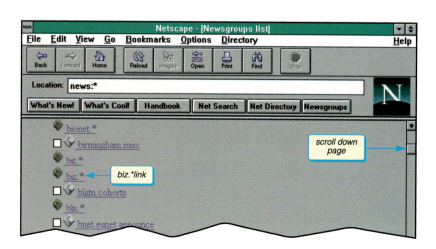

FIGURE 2-63

STEP 2 ▶

Click the biz.* link.

A Newsgroups list page containing an outlined list of biz news groups displays (Figure 2-64). The groups are in alphabetical order. The biz.jobs.offered link is further down the page.

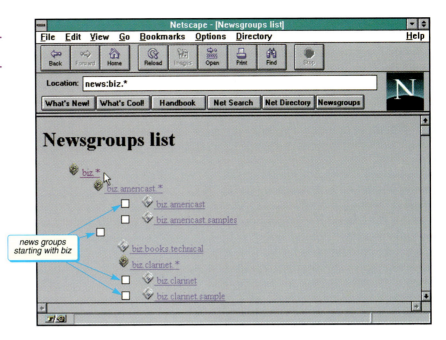

FIGURE 2-64

STEP 3 ▶

Scroll down the page until the biz.jobs.offered link displays (Figure 2-65).

The biz.jobs.offered link links to jobs news groups.

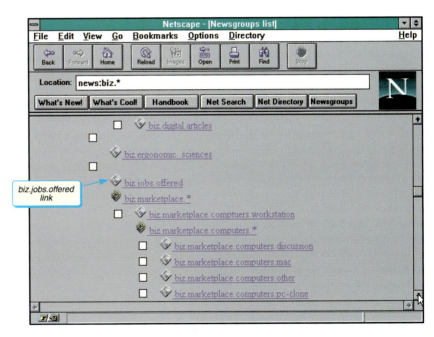

FIGURE 2-65

STEP 4 ▶

Click the biz.jobs.offered link.

The Newsgroup: biz.jobs.offered article summary page displays (Figure 2-66). The page contains a list of available articles to be read.

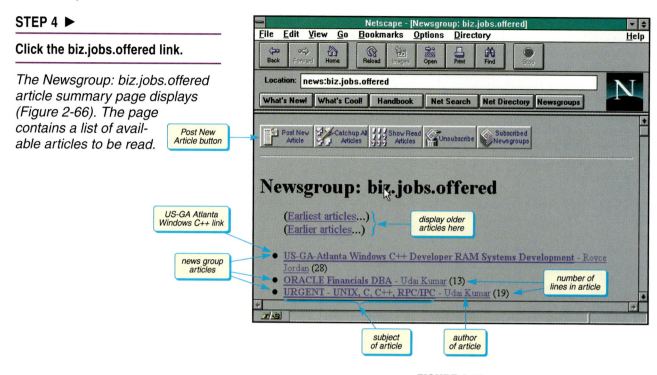

FIGURE 2-66

The links with the larger round bullets next to them are individual news group articles. Notice you can get older articles than the ones on the page by clicking one of the two links at the top of the page.

The buttons at the top of the page allow you to post a new article to the news group, manage articles, and subscribe or unsubscribe to the news group. You will use the Post New Article button to send your own news group article later in the project.

Reading News Group Articles

Each link on the article summary page in Figure 2-66 reflects the contents of the subject line that appears inside the article. This is so you can look at the subjects of the articles to decide if you want to read them without actually having to display the article. The author of the article and the number of lines in the article display after the link. You can now read an article, as shown in the following steps.

TO READ A NEWS GROUP ARTICLE ▼

STEP 1 ▶

Click the US-GA-Atlanta Windows C++ link.

The news article displays (Figure 2-67). An article toolbar displays at the top of the article, followed by the article heading.

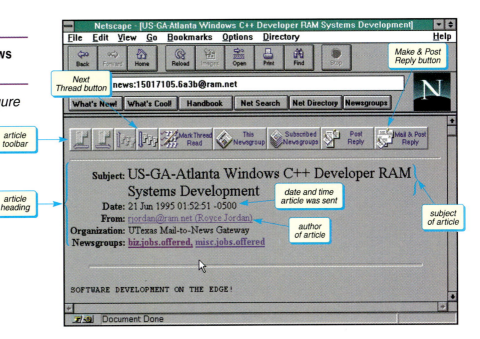

FIGURE 2-67

STEP 2 ▶

Scroll down the page.

The body of the article displays (Figure 2-68). It is here that the duties and minimum requirements for the job are explained in detail.

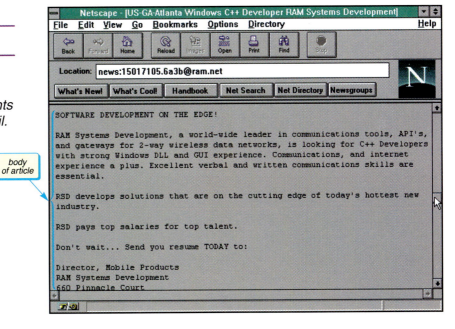

FIGURE 2-68

Notice in Figure 2-67 on the previous page the article toolbar at the top of the page. Table 2-4 summarizes the functions of the buttons. This toolbar also will appear at the bottom of the article page.

Next comes the heading of the article. The heading contains the subject of the article, the date and time the article was posted, the person who posted the article, and the organization from which the article was sent. Following the heading is the body, which contains the contents of the article.

▶ **TABLE 2-4**

TOOLBAR BUTTON	BUTTON FUNCTION
	Displays previous article in the thread
	Displays the next article in the thread
	Displays the first article from the previous thread
	Displays the first article from the next thread
Mark Thread Read	Marks all articles in the current thread as read
This Newsgroup	Returns to the article summary list for the current news group
Subscribed Newsgroups	Returns to the Subscribed Newsgroup page
Post Reply	Replies to an article
Mail & Post Reply	Replies to an article and sends private electronic mail messages

After reading this article, you can move to the next article in the news group by pressing the applicable button on the article toolbar, as shown in the following steps.

TO READ THE NEXT NEWS GROUP ARTICLE ▼

STEP 1 ▶

Scroll to the top of the article until the article toolbar displays. Click the Next Thread button (▨) on the article toolbar.

The next article in the news group displays (Figure 2-69).

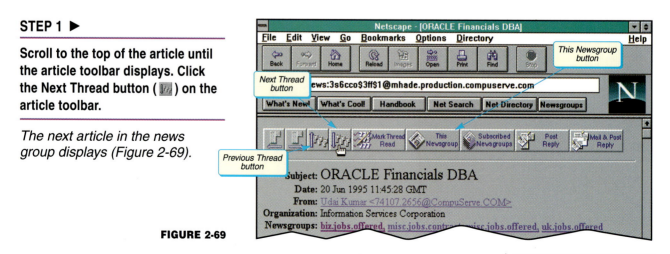

FIGURE 2-69

Notice the icon in the Previous Thread button on the article toolbar turns blue. This is because you left the previous thread, which consisted of just one article, and moved to the current thread. Clicking this button returns you to the US-GA-Atlanta Windows C++ article.

Saving and Printing News Group Articles

You will almost certainly want to save news articles on a diskette that contain interesting or important information. Saving articles is accomplished the same way as saving any other hypertext page in Netscape. Printing articles is also accomplished the same way as printing a hypertext page.

Redisplaying the News Group Article Summary Page

You can continue reading, saving, or printing each of the articles in the biz.jobs.offered news group. You can also skip around among the articles in the news group by redisplaying the biz.jobs.offered article summary page and selecting a specific article to display. The following step shows how to redisplay the news group article summary page.

TO REDISPLAY THE BIZ.JOBS.OFFERED ARTICLE SUMMARY PAGE ▼

STEP 1 ▶

Click the This Newsgroup button (This Newsgroup) on the article toolbar.

The biz.jobs.offered article summary page displays (Figure 2-70). The visited links change color, indicating the articles have been read.

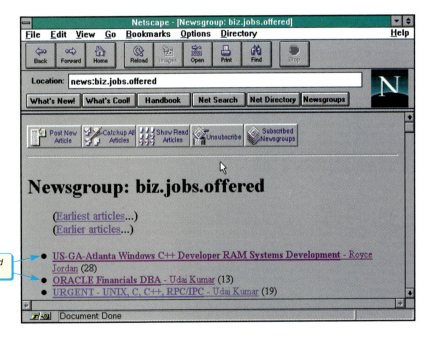

FIGURE 2-70

Now you can choose another article to display from Newsgroup: biz.jobs.offered.

Redisplaying the List of News Groups

When you are finished reading the articles, you must leave this news group and select another before you can read those articles. The following steps show how to redisplay the list of news groups to select another.

TO REDISPLAYING THE LIST OF NEWS GROUPS ▼

STEP 1 ▶

Click the Back button on the Netscape toolbar.

The outlined list of biz. news groups displays.

STEP 2 ▶

Click the Back button on the Netscape toolbar again.

The Newsgroups list page redisplays (Figure 2-71).

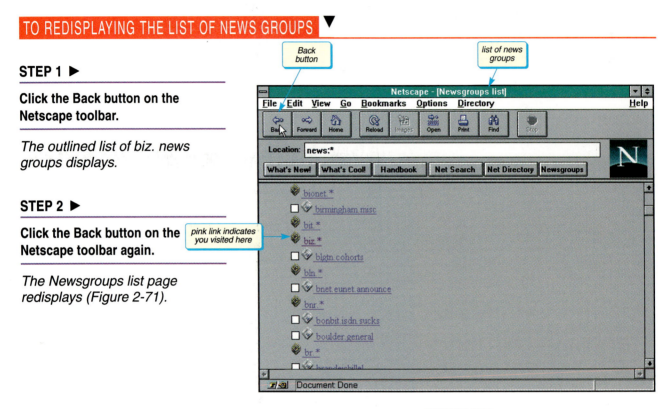

FIGURE 2-71

You can now select another news group to visit. You have learned how to display, save, and print individual news group articles and move to another news group.

Posting News Group Articles

News groups contain a treasure chest of information and amusement. It is likely a time may come when you will want to post, or send, an article to a news group. The following steps show how to submit a news group article by posting to the news.test news group. This is a news group just for testing purposes. This way, you will not disturb any other news group participants with your practice articles. When you are familiar with the posting process, you can select an appropriate news group to send your thoughts and opinions.

TO POST A NEWS GROUP ARTICLE ▼

STEP 1 ▶

Scroll down the list of news groups until the news.* link displays (Figure 2-72).

In the news. link, the news group news.test is found.*

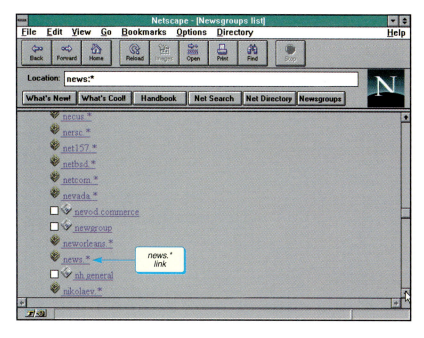

FIGURE 2-72

STEP 2 ▶

Click the news.* link. Scroll down to the bottom of the news.* Newsgroups list page (Figure 2-73).

Notice the facilities for searching news groups, obtaining an up-to-date list of news groups, and subscribing to selected news groups. Subscribing will be illustrated later in the project.

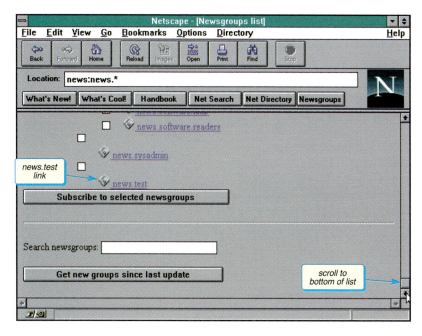

FIGURE 2-73

STEP 3 ▶

Click the news.test link.

The news.test article summary page displays (Figure 2-74). Notice several test articles on this page.

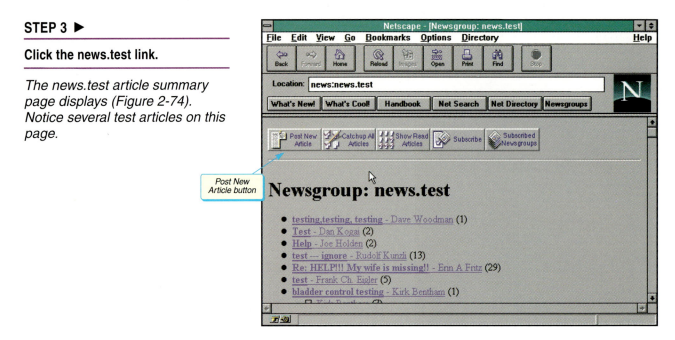

FIGURE 2-74

STEP 4 ▶

Click the Post New Article button ( ) on the article toolbar.

The Send Mail/Post News dialog box displays (Figure 2-75). This page serves two purposes, posting news articles and sending electronic mail. Sending electronic mail will be covered later in this project. Text fields provide information for the article heading and the article body. At the bottom of the form are buttons for canceling the operation, including the current page in the display area in the article and sending the article to the news group.

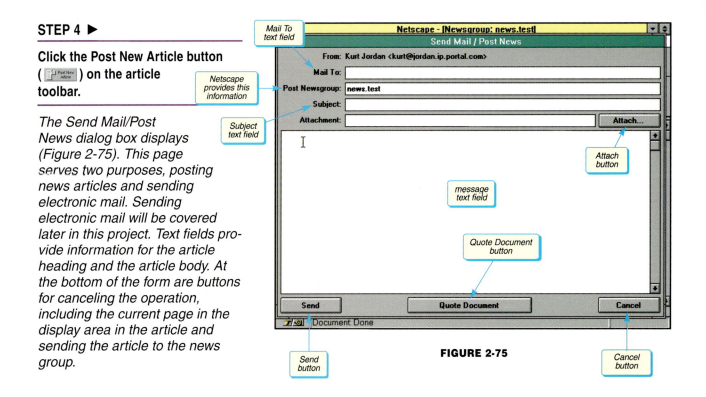

FIGURE 2-75

STEP 5 ▶

Press the TAB key until the insertion point displays in the Subject text field. Type test news posting **(Figure 2-76).**

This is the subject of the article. Recall that subjects are important parts of Internet communications.

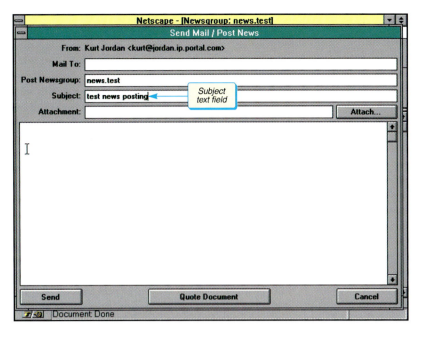

FIGURE 2-76

STEP 6 ▶

Press the TAB key until the insertion point displays in the message field where the body of the article will be typed. Type I like looking through all the different news group articles. **(Figure 2-77).**

STEP 7 ▶

Click the Send button.

The news.test article summary page redisplays, as shown in Figure 2-74. Other people with news group access can now read your article.

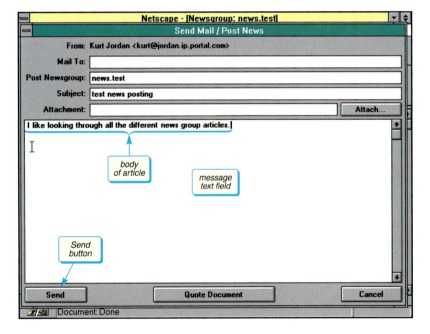

FIGURE 2-77

▲

You can also move between the fields by clicking the mouse pointer within each text field. The insertion point will display, and you can type in the information.

You learned how to post a new article to a news group. You can now return to the list of news groups and select another to read or to post to.

Subscribing to News Groups

Remember that the list of news groups is very large, with thousands of news groups. Having to retrieve, and then scroll through the list whenever you want to access your favorite news groups can get tiresome, and wastes time. You can instruct Netscape to store a list of your favorite news groups and present them each time you go to read news. You can then choose from among this short list, and proceed directly to read the articles that interest you the most.

The list of news groups is stored on a disk file called newsrc. The process of building this list is called **subscribing**. You can include new, interesting news groups you find, and remove old ones that no longer interest you. The following steps illustrate how to subscribe to the news.test news group.

TO SUBSCRIBE TO A NEWS GROUP ▼

STEP 1 ▶

Click the Back button on the Netscape toolbar.

The outlined list of news.* news groups displays.

STEP 2 ▶

Click the small white check box above and to the left of the news.test link.

An x appears in the check box (Figure 2-78), indicating this news group has been selected.

FIGURE 2-78

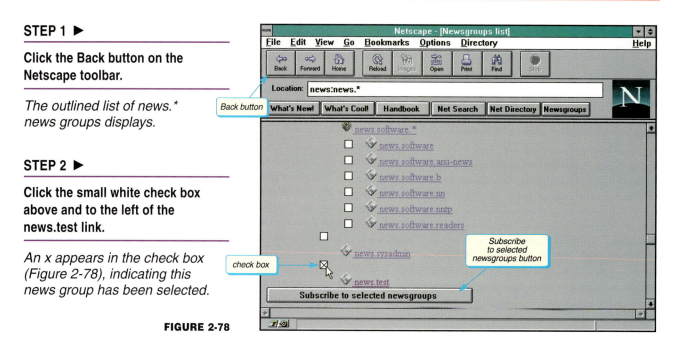

STEP 3 ▶

Click the Subscribe to selected newsgroups button.

The Subscribed newsgroups page redisplays, with the newly subscribed news group added to the list (Figure 2-79). Notice the news.test link appears at the bottom of the list. The news.test link is pink because you visited that link earlier when posting a news group article.

FIGURE 2-79

Now when you access news groups from within Netscape, this list will appear after you select a USENET host, and you can proceed right to your favorite news groups without having to retrieve the long list of news groups. You can click the boxes of several news groups and subscribe to them all at once by pressing the Subscribe to selected newsgroup button.

Unsubscribing from a News Group

When you no longer want a particular news group to appear in your list of subscribed news groups, you can remove the news group from the newsrc file. This process is called **unsubscribing**. The following steps show how to unsubscribe from the news.test news group.

TO UNSUBSCRIBE FROM A NEWS GROUP

STEP 1 ▶

Click the news.test check box.

An x appears in the check box (Figure 2-80). Selecting this check box indicates this news group has been selected.

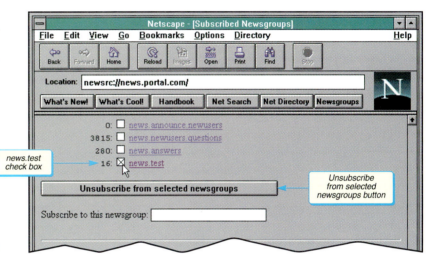

FIGURE 2-80

STEP 2 ▶

Click the Unsubscribe from selected newsgroups button.

The Subscribed newsgroups page redisplays (Figure 2-81). Notice the news.test link is now gone.

FIGURE 2-81

You have learned how to display lists of news groups, read and post articles, and subscribe to and unsubscribe from news groups.

Articles posted to news groups can be read by anyone who has access to the news groups and has Netscape or some other news reader program. What if you wanted to respond privately to the author of a news article? Netscape has the capability of sending private messages to individuals over the Internet using an Internet service called electronic mail.

▶ ELECTRONIC MAIL

Probably the most popular service on the Internet is **electronic mail**, or **e-mail**. Using e-mail, you can converse with individuals across the room or on another continent.

Corresponding with electronic mail consists of composing and sending messages to others, and managing the messages that others send to you. Netscape is a marvelous tool for using Internet services, including composing and sending messages to other people on the Internet. It does not, however, have any facilities for receiving, reading, or managing the messages that others send to you.

Because of this, the following sections show how to send electronic mail using Netscape, and how to read and manage mail messages you receive using a popular Windows electronic mail program called Eudora.

▶ PREPARING TO USE NETSCAPE FOR ELECTRONIC MAIL

Before sending a mail message over the Internet, you must know the recipient's electronic mail address. An individual's **electronic mail address** consists of an account name followed by the @ character, then the Internet address (or domain name) of the remote computer where the person's account is located (Figure 2-82).

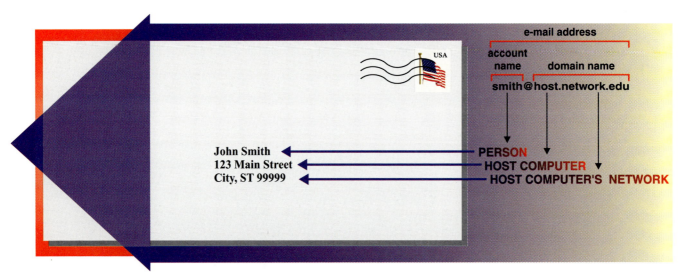

FIGURE 2-82

In addition, you must provide your electronic mail address in a special form before Netscape will allow you to send mail. The following steps show how to enter your e-mail address in the Netscape form.

TO PROVIDE YOUR E-MAIL ADDRESS TO NETSCAPE ▼

STEP 1 ▶

Select the Options menu, and choose the Preferences command.

The Preferences dialog box displays (Figure 2-83). Several different settings affecting how Netscape performs can be changed in this dialog box.

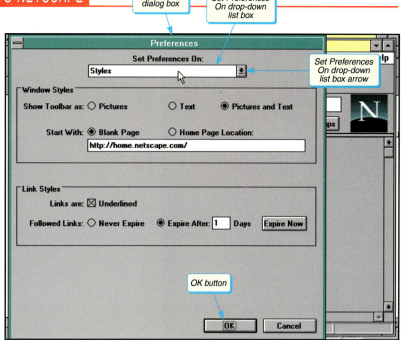

FIGURE 2-83

STEP 2 ▶

Click the Set Preferences On drop-down list box arrow.

The Set Preferences On drop-down list box displays (Figure 2-84). Each entry in the Set Preferences On list box represents a number of different setting you can use to customize Netscape. The Mail and News preference performs electronic mail setup.

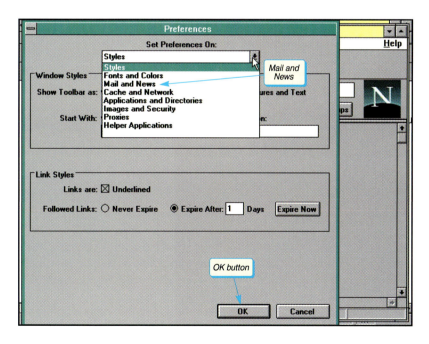

FIGURE 2-84

STEP 3 ▶

Click Mail and News.

The Mail and News input form in the Preferences dialog box displays (Figure 2-85).

STEP 4 ▶

Drag the mouse pointer over the electronic mail address in the Your Email text box and type your electronic mail address. Drag the mouse pointer over the name in the Your Name text box and type your full name. Choose the OK button in the Preferences dialog box.

The dialog box will disappear. If you do not have an electronic mail address, ask your instructor what the address is.

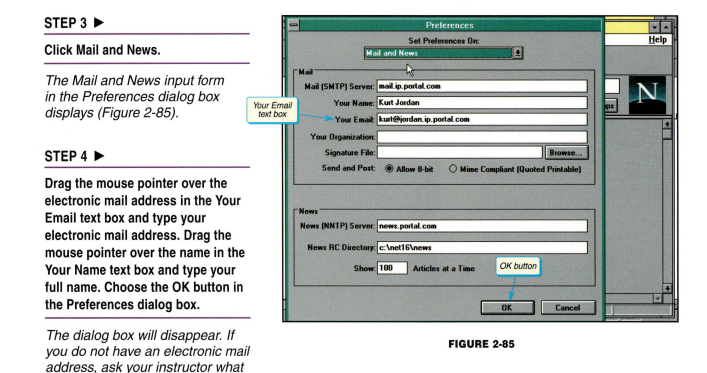

FIGURE 2-85

Your e-mail address will stay in Netscape until you or someone else changes it. Be careful not to change other settings in the dialog box. Changing settings could cause mail and news groups not to function. You can now send mail using the Mail form provided by Netscape.

Sending a Mail Message Using Netscape

When sending mail, you must provide the recipient's e-mail address, a brief one-line sentence, called the subject, that identifies the purpose or contents of the message, and the message itself.

The message will then be sent over the Internet. When it arrives at its destination, the destination computer stores the message in a special file using the receiver's account name as the filename. This file is the **mail box**. The messages will stay in the mail box until the receiver starts a mail program, such as Eudora, and reads the incoming mail. The mail program will open the mail box and allow the individual to issue commands to read, save, delete, print, or otherwise manage electronic mail.

The following steps illustrate how to send a mail message to yourself. For you to successfully carry out these steps, you should substitute your electronic mail address wherever you see kurt@jordan.ip.portal.com. The message will then be sent to your account. This is to ensure you will have a mail message to use while continuing through the section on e-mail in this project. If you do not have an electronic mail address, ask your instructor for information on how to obtain a mail account.

TO SEND A MAIL MESSAGE ▼

STEP 1 ▶

Select the File menu.

The File menu displays (Figure 2-86).

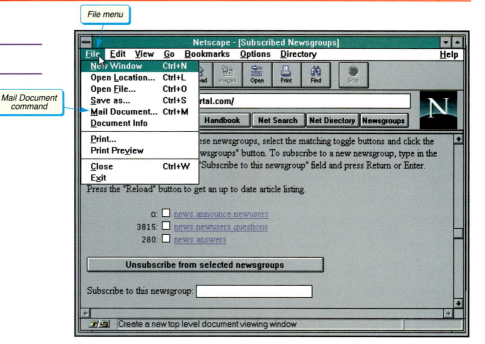

FIGURE 2-86

STEP 2 ▶

Choose Mail Document command.

The Send Mail/Post News dialog box displays (Figure 2-87). This is the same dialog box you used to post a news group article. Notice the text fields where you enter the electronic mail address of the recipient, the subject of the message, any files you want to attach to the message, and a large message field for the message itself. The insertion point is in the Mail To text field. The URL in the Subject text field is the URL from the news group page in the display area.

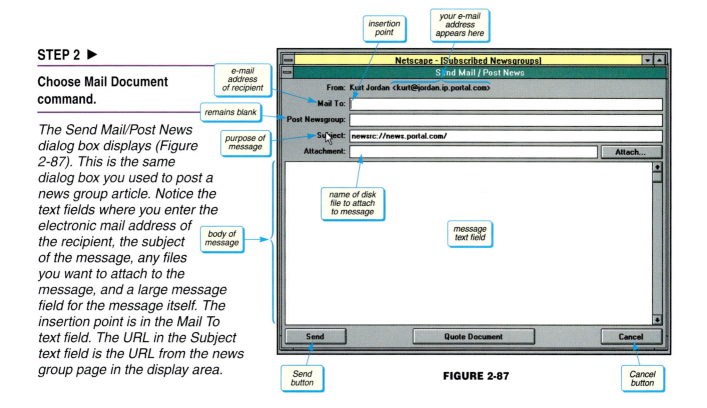

FIGURE 2-87

STEP 3 ▶

With the insertion point in the Mail to: box, type your e-mail address. Press the TAB key to move the insertion point past the Post Newsgroup text field to the Subject text field. Type Computer games book **(Figure 2-88).**

The Post Newsgroup text field is left blank because you are not sending a news group article.

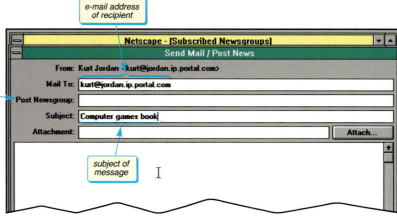

FIGURE 2-88

STEP 4 ▶

Press the TAB key to move past the Attachment: box, to the large message text box. Type I found a book on computer games. It's called Action Arcade Adventure Set. It comes with a diskette that has all you need to get started writing games. I'll let you know if it is any good. Bye. **(Figure 2-89).**

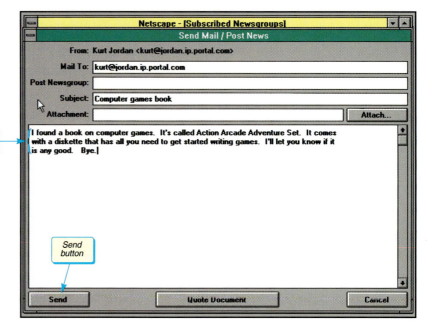

FIGURE 2-89

STEP 5 ▶

Click the Send button at the bottom of the screen.

The Send Mail/Post News dialog box disappears, and a Document Done message appears in the status line, indicating the message has been sent (Figure 2-90).

Here are the newsgroups to which you are currently subscribed. The number to the left of the newsgroup name is how many unread articles currently exist in that group.

To unsubscribe from any of these newsgroups, select the matching toggle buttons and click the "Unsubscribe from selected newsgroups" button. To subscribe to a new newsgroup, type in the name of the newsgroup in the "Subscribe to this newsgroup" field and press Return or Enter.

Press the "Reload" button to get an up to date article listing.

    0: ☐ news.announce.newusers
3815: ☐ news.newusers.questions
  280: ☐ news.answers

Unsubscribe from selected newsgroups

 Document Done

message was sent

FIGURE 2-90

It is important to correctly indicate the content or purpose of the message in the subject line, not only when using electronic mail, but also in other Internet correspondence. This allows the recipient to categorize and screen mail without having to read each message. If your subject is vague, or missing, people may just delete the message without reading it.

You can move around within the message, making any desired corrections before clicking the Send button. The message text field will scroll down, allowing more room for typing longer messages.

Adding Personality to Your Mail Messages

Even though the person reading your mail messages might be on the other side of the world, you can still convey your personality and emotions along with the message. This is accomplished by including special combinations of characters, called **smiley faces**, or **smileys** in your message. Table 2-5 contains several smiley faces and their meanings. The first smiley in Table 2-5 consists of three characters: a colon (:), a minus sign (-), and a right parenthesis ( )).

In addition to the smiley faces, several other character combinations, intended to save time and space, have become popular on the Internet. These combinations are abbreviations of frequently used phrases. Table 2-6 shows some of the more popular abbreviations.

▸ **TABLE 2-5**

SMILEY	MEANING
:-)	I'm happy / I'm smiling
:-(	I'm sad / I'm unhappy
;-)	Conveys sarcasm
0 :-)	An angelic or innocent remark
:-D	I'm laughing
:-O	I'm surprised

Reading Electronic Mail Using Eudora

Although Netscape has no facilities for receiving or reading mail, several other programs are available to read your e-mail messages. One of the more popular Windows programs for managing electronic mail is **Eudora**.

Eudora is available from several public access FTP sites. You obtained a copy of Eudora previously in the section on FTP on page N79. If your school does not have Eudora available, follow the instructions in Appendix B to load it on your computer system.

▸ **TABLE 2-6**

ABBREVIATION	MEANING
ASAP	As soon as possible
BTW	By the way
CU	See you later
IMHO	In my humble opinion
NRN	No reply necessary
PLS	Please
THX	Thank you

Starting Eudora

Once Eudora is properly installed, start it using the same steps as for other Windows applications, as shown on the next page.

TO START EUDORA ▼

STEP 1 ▶

If Netscape is on the screen, press ALT+TAB to return to Program Manager. Use the mouse pointer to point to the Eudora program-item icon in the EMAIL group window (Figure 2-91).

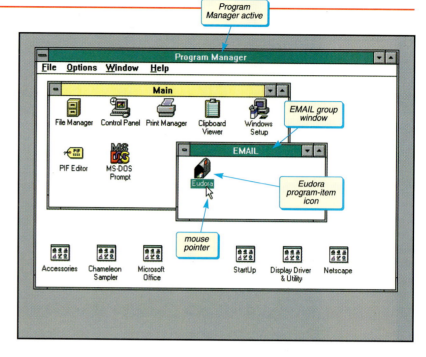

FIGURE 2-91

STEP 2 ▶

Double-click the left mouse button.

The Eudora window displays (Figure 2-92). The Eudora window contains a menu bar and an In mail box containing a toolbar.

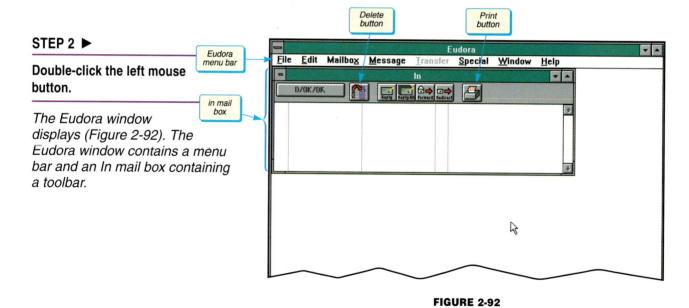

FIGURE 2-92

Notice there are no mail messages in the In mail box, even though you sent a message to yourself using Netscape in previous steps in Project 2. This is because the computer where mail is stored, the **mail server**, holds mail boxes for many different people. You have to identify yourself to the mail server so it can deliver your mail to you, as shown in the following steps.

TO CONTACT THE MAIL SERVER ▼

STEP 1 ►

Select the File menu.

The File menu displays (Figure 2-93). Only certain commands are available. The Check Mail command is one.

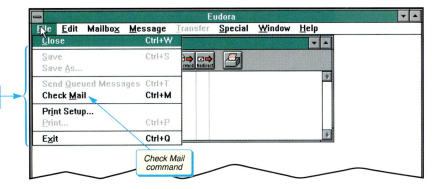

FIGURE 2-93

STEP 2 ►

Choose the Check Mail command.

The Enter Password dialog box displays (Figure 2-94). In the Password text box, you provide the password for your e-mail account. If you do not know your password, see your instructor for information on how to obtain one.

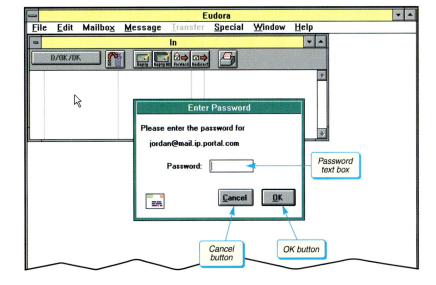

FIGURE 2-94

STEP 3 ►

Enter the password in the Password text box for your mail account and choose the OK button.

The Eudora dialog box displays indicating you have new mail (Figure 2-95). Notice the new message in the In mail box.

STEP 4 ►

Choose the OK button in the Eudora dialog box.

The dialog box disappears.

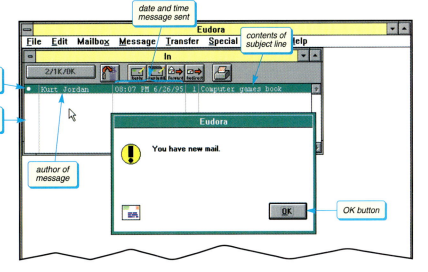

FIGURE 2-95

Each line in the In mail box contains the name of the author of the message, the date and time the message was sent, and the contents of the subject line of the message. You can see how important the subject is when composing a message. Other people reading their mail will browse through the subjects, deciding which messages to read, and which to disregard. If your subject is vague, or missing, chances are no one will read your message.

Other messages might appear in the list of messages. Some colleges and organizations send a welcome mail message to an account when it is first created. You might see this welcome message in the summary list. One of your friends could have sent you a mail message already. Make note of the Computer games book message and use it as you continue with the project.

Reading Mail Messages

You can now read the Computer games book message in the In mail box, as shown in the following step.

TO READ A MAIL MESSAGE IN EUDORA ▼

STEP 1 ▶

Click the line containing the Computer games book subject.

The mail message appears (Figure 2-96). The message consists of a message heading and a message body.

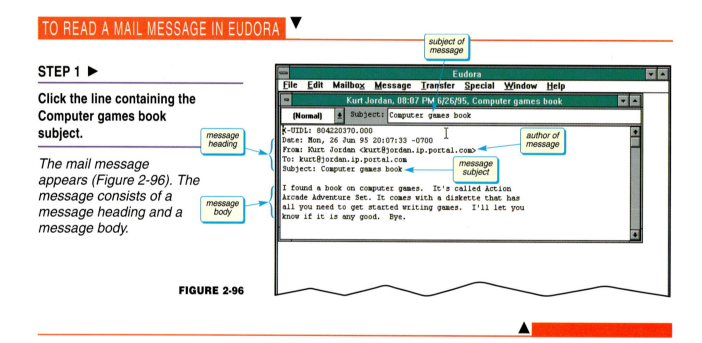

FIGURE 2-96

The message is made up of two parts. The first part consists of the message heading, containing the author of the message, the date and time the message was sent, the recipient of the message, and the subject line. The second part contains the body of the message. If the message is larger than the message field, you can scroll down the window, revealing more of the message.

Saving a Message on a Diskette

Some messages you receive may be so important that you will want to save them on a diskette. For example, a message may contain program source code, or answers to a problem that you will want for future reference. Perhaps you just want to preserve a record, or **audit trail**, of your correspondence. The following steps illustrate how to save the Computer games book mail message on a diskette in drive A.

TO SAVE A MAIL MESSAGE ON A DISKETTE ▼

STEP 1 ▶

Insert a formatted diskette
in drive A.

STEP 2 ▶

Select the File menu.

*The File menu displays (Figure
2-97). The Save As command is
active.*

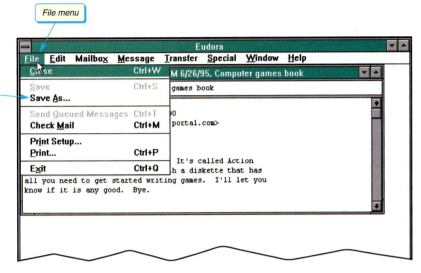

FIGURE 2-97

STEP 3 ▶

Choose the Save As command.
Click the Drives drop-down list box
arrow. Click the drive A icon.

*The Save As dialog box displays
(Figure 2-98).*

STEP 4 ▶

Choose the OK button in the Save
As dialog box to save the message.

*The Save As dialog box will
disappear.*

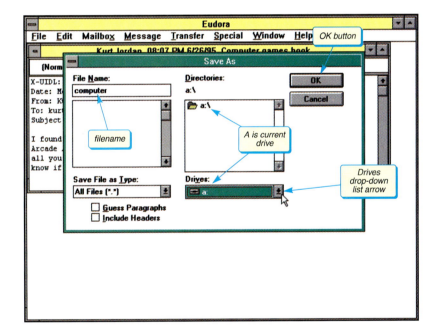

FIGURE 2-98

The message has been saved to the diskette in drive A in a file called
computer.

Printing a Mail Message

Eudora provides facilities for printing mail messages through the Print
command on the File menu.

TO PRINT A MAIL MESSAGE ▼

STEP 1 ▶

Ready the printer according to the printer instructions.

STEP 2 ▶

Select the File menu and choose the Print command.

The Print dialog box displays (Figure 2-99).

STEP 3 ▶

Choose the OK button in the Print dialog box.

The Printing Progress box will display. When printing is complete, the box disappears.

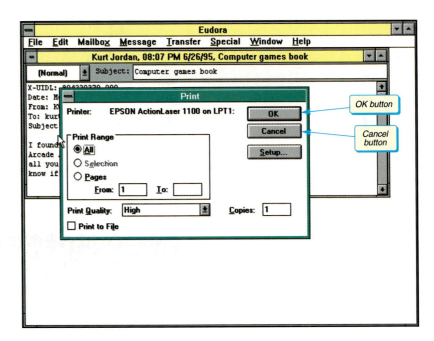

FIGURE 2-99

The printed message contains both the message heading and message body. You can also print a message in the In mail box by highlighting the message and clicking the Print button on the toolbar as shown in Figure 2-92 on page N108.

Deleting a Mail Message

Once you have read, and possibly saved a message, you should remove unwanted mail messages from the In mail box. If you do not delete mail messages, the list of messages will get very long. In addition, allowing old messages to accumulate in your mail box wastes disk space. The following steps delete the Computer games book mail message.

TO DELETE A MAIL MESSAGE ▼

STEP 1 ▶

Select the Message menu.

The Message menu displays (Figure 2-100). Most of the commands are available, including Reply, Forward, New Message, and Delete.

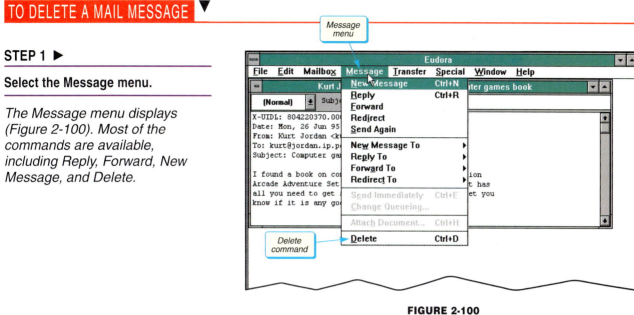

FIGURE 2-100

STEP 2 ▶

Choose the Delete command.

The message display window disappears. The Computer games book message has been removed from the In mail box window (Figure 2-101).

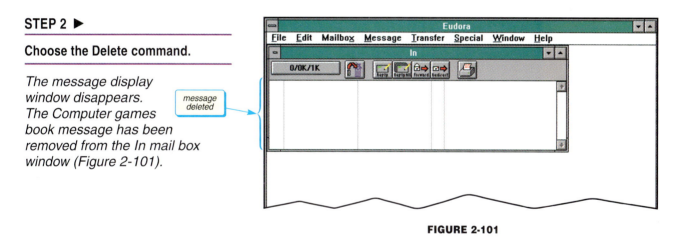

FIGURE 2-101

▲

You can continue to read, save, print, and delete other messages you may receive.

Exiting Eudora

When you are finished managing your mail, use the following steps to exit Eudora.

TO EXIT EUDORA

Step 1: Select the File menu.
Step 2: Choose the Exit command.

The Program manager window displays, as shown in Figure 2-91 on page N108.

▶ PROJECT SUMMARY

In this project, you learned how to search the World Wide Web using InfoSeek, WebCrawler and the Yahoo Directory. You also learned how to retrieve files with FTP and gopher and how to send and read news group articles. Finally, you learned how to send electronic mail messages from Netscape and how to read, save, print, and delete electronic mail messages using Eudora.

▶ KEY TERMS AND INDEX

audit trail *(N110)*
current directory *(N75)*
electronic mail (e-mail) *(N102)*
electronic mail address *(N102)*
e-mail *(N102)*
Eudora *(N107)*
File Transfer Protocol (FTP) *(N73)*
FTP archives *(N73)*
gopher *(N82)*
InfoSeek *(N58)*

keyword *(N56)*
mail box *(N104)*
mail server *(N108)*
news groups *(N87)*
post *(N87)*
pub *(N75)*
repositories *(N73)*
search engine *(N56)*
search tools *(N56)*
selectable map *(N70)*

smiley faces *(N107)*
smileys *(N107)*
subscribed *(N88)*
subscribing *(N100)*
thread *(N87)*
unsubscribing *(N101)*
USENET *(N87)*
viewers *(N80)*
WebCrawler *(N63)*
Yahoo Directory *(N68)*

S T U D E N T   A S S I G N M E N T S

STUDENT ASSIGNMENT 1
True/False

Instructions: Circle T if the statement is true or F if the statement is false.

T F 1. Web search tools allow you to search in terms of where a file is located.

T F 2. All Web search tools perform the same type of search.

T F 3. With WebCrawler, when you type more than one keyword in the text box, you can control whether both must appear in the Web page, or whether one or the other must appear in the Web page.

T F 4. When adjusting the number of results to return in WebCrawler, you can type any number you want.

T F 5. WebCrawler search results include a relevance score.

T F 6. InfoSeek uses a series of menus to organize links to Web pages.

T F 7. The Yahoo directory is accessed by pressing the Internet Directory button.

T F 8. The second most popular activity on the Internet is electronic mail.

T F 9. The FTP (File Transfer Protocol) program moves files between computers.

T F 10. FTP sites do not have a URL you can use to access them.

T F 11. The icons on the FTP directory pages identify the types of files found there.

T F 12. Most FTP sites organize their files into directories using some logical technique, such as operating system name, or software topic.

T F 13. A way to determine the contents of files at popular FTP sites is not available.

T   F   14. Gopher started out as a document creation system.
T   F   15. Gopher menus have icons similar to FTP directory pages.
T   F   16. A very large number of electronic discussion groups called news groups are available on the Internet.
T   F   17. You can generally determine the topic of discussion you will find in a news group by looking at its name.
T   F   18. Netscape has facilities for sending and receiving electronic mail.
T   F   19. An electronic mail address consists of an individual's account name, followed by the & character, and then the Internet address or domain name of the remote computer.
T   F   20. It is not important to have a good subject in your messages because no one reads the subjects anyway.

STUDENT ASSIGNMENT 2
Multiple Choice

Instructions: Circle the correct response.

1. The search engine that allows you to alter the number of URLs returned is _____.
   a. Eudora
   b. Yahoo Directory
   c. InfoSeek
   d. WebCrawler
2. The search engine that uses a list of general categories from which you repeatedly select a topic is called _____.
   a. Eudora
   b. Yahoo Directory
   c. InfoSeek
   d. WebCrawler
3. The letters FTP stand for _____.
   a. File Transfer Protocol
   b. Find the Program
   c. File Transport Program
   d. they do not stand for anything
4. The name of that portion of the disk where the user is located in a FTP site's directory structure is called _____.
   a. a Web page
   b. the URL
   c. the thread
   d. the current directory
5. The collection of computers that store and make available news groups is called _____.
   a. a thread
   b. FTP archive
   c. USENET
   d. the Internet
6. Access to news groups is achieved by clicking the _____ button.
   a. Net Search
   b. Newsgroups
   c. Back
   d. Net Directory

(continued)

STUDENT ASSIGNMENT 2 (continued)

7. Adding a news group to the newsrc file is called _____.
   a. unsubscribing
   b. subscribing
   c. posting
   d. saving

8. The place where mail messages are stored until they are read is called _____.
   a. a thread
   b. a diskette
   c. newsrc
   d. a mail box

9. Special combinations of characters called _____ help convey emotion and personality.
   a. abbreviations
   b. smileys
   c. frowns
   d. remarks

10. A(n) _____ is a preserved record of your mail correspondence.
   a. audit trail
   b. file on a diskette
   c. thread
   d. mail box

STUDENT ASSIGNMENT 3
Understanding Mail Message Headings

Instructions: Figure SA2-3 contains a sample mail message. Answer the questions regarding the message header in the spaces provided at the top of the next page.

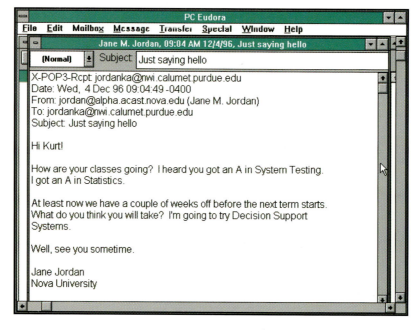

FIGURE SA2-3

1. Who sent the message?

   _____

2. Who received the message?

   _____

3. What is the message subject?

   _____

4. When was this message sent?

   _____

5. Do you think the subject was descriptive enough? Why or why not?

   _____

   _____

STUDENT ASSIGNMENT 4
Practicing Writing Subjects

Instructions: Write a short descriptive subject for each of the following messages.

1. Fourth-quarter results for XYZ Corporation were impressive, with revenues increasing 23% over the same quarter last year. Long-term debt is low. I would strongly suggest purchasing more of this rapidly growing company.

   _____

2. There are several places you can find directories and indexes to Internet resources. These directories can be obtained using gopher or FTP. One notable directory is the Internet Resources Guide, located at the una.hh.lib.umich.edu in the /inetdirs directory.

   _____

3. Hi Jane! How are classes going? I hope everything is fine. How do you like dorm life? The cats are doing OK. Crusty still beats up on the others. He's so fat! It's a wonder he can catch them. Thanks for sending me that tax program. It came in real handy. Well, gotta go. Bye.

   _____

4. The CU-SeeMe system, developed at Cornell University, lets you broadcast yourself all over the Internet. All you need is a small video camera and video card, which are available at most computer stores for a few hundred dollars. The display is a bit jerky, but fun to experiment with.

   _____

STUDENT ASSIGNMENT 5
Understanding News Group Article Toolbar Buttons

Instructions: In Figure SA2-5, arrows point to several buttons on the article toolbar. In the spaces provided, briefly explain the purpose of each button.

FIGURE SA2-5

STUDENT ASSIGNMENT 6
Understanding the Send Mail/Post News Form

Instructions: In Figure SA2-6, arrows point to the text fields in the Send Mail/Post News dialog box. In the spaces provided, briefly explain the purpose of each text field.

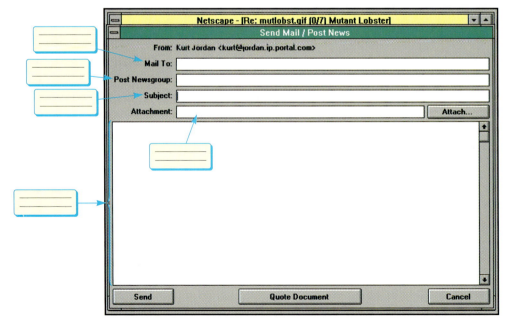

FIGURE SA2-6

HANDS-ON EXERCISE 1
Obtaining Help for Web Search Tools

Purpose: To understand how to obtain more information about using the Web search engines.

Instructions: Start Netscape and perform the following tasks with a computer.

1. Click the Net Search directory button.
2. Scroll down to the InfoSeek form.
3. Click the special query operators link.
4. Print the Web page containing the searching techniques explanations.
5. Return to the Internet Search page.
6. Scroll down to the WebCrawler link and click the link.
7. Scroll down to the hints link at the bottom of the WebCrawler page and click the link.
8. Print the WebCrawler hints page.
9. Write a brief comparison of InfoSeek and WebCrawler search techniques.
10. Turn in all printouts to your instructor.

HANDS-ON EXERCISE 2
Searching the Web with InfoSeek

Purpose: To understand how to search the Web using InfoSeek.

Instructions: Start Netscape and perform the following tasks with a computer.

1. Select the following topics one at a time: geology; ocean; fungus; molecule; tiddlywinks; shark.
2. Using InfoSeek, perform a search on the topic.
3. Print the page of Search Results and turn it in to your instructor.

HANDS-ON EXERCISE 3
Searching the Web with WebCrawler

Purpose: To understand how to search the Web using WebCrawler.

Instructions: Start Netscape and perform the following tasks with a computer.

1. Select the following topics one at a time: gorilla; football; cloud; rock; engine; baby.
2. Using WebCrawler, perform a search on the topic.
3. Select one of the links returned and follow it until you find a picture of your topic (Figure HOE2-3 on the next page).

(continued)

HANDS–ON EXERCISE 3 (continued)

FIGURE HOE2-3

4. Print a picture for each topic, and turn it in to your instructor.

<h2 style="text-align:center">HANDS-ON EXERCISE 4
Retrieving a File Using FTP</h2>

Purpose: To understand how to retrieve files using FTP.

Instructions: To view movies, listen to sound clips, and handle other types of special files, Netscape uses special programs called helper applications. One special type of file is called mpeg. It contains a short movie, sometimes accompanied by sound. To view mpeg files, you need a mpeg helper application. Start Netscape and perform the following tasks to retrieve a mpeg movie viewer.

1. Using FTP, connect to ftp.ncsa.uiuc.edu.
2. Move to the /Mosaic/Windows/viewers directory.
3. Retrieve the files mpegw32h.zip and unzip.exe.
4. Unzip the mpeg viewer and install it in Windows. Follow the steps outlined in Appendix B, substituting the mpegw32h.zip filename whenever the eudor144.zip filename displays.
5. Return to Netscape and connect to http://www.acm.uiuc.edu:80/rml/Mpeg.
6. Scroll down the page and retrieve an mpeg movie to play with your viewer similar to the one in Figure HOE2-4.

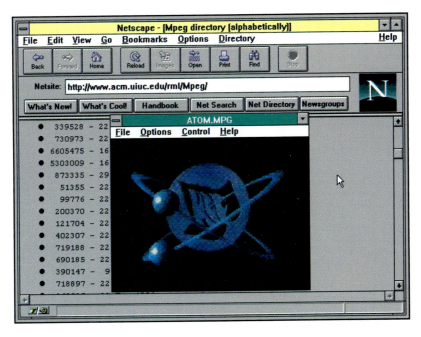

FIGURE HOE2-4

HANDS-ON EXERCISE 5
Retrieving Files Using Gopher

Purpose: To understand how to retrieve files using gopher.

Instructions: Start Netscape and perform the following tasks with a computer.

1. Connect to gopher://wiretap.spies.com (Figure HOE2-5).

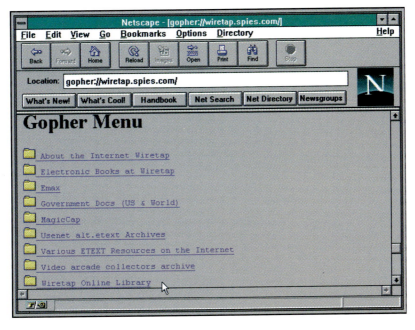

FIGURE HOE2-5

(continued)

HANDS–ON EXERCISE 5 (continued)

2. Click Wiretap Online Library.
3. Click Articles.
4. Click Food and Drink.
5. Select one of the recipes and save it on a diskette in drive A.
6. Print the recipe and turn it in to your instructor.

HANDS-ON EXERCISE 6
Reading News Group Articles

Purpose: To understand how to read news group articles.

Instructions: Start Netscape and perform the following tasks with a computer.

1. Select the Directory menu and choose the Go To Newsgroups command.
2. Display the list of news groups (Figure HOE2-6).

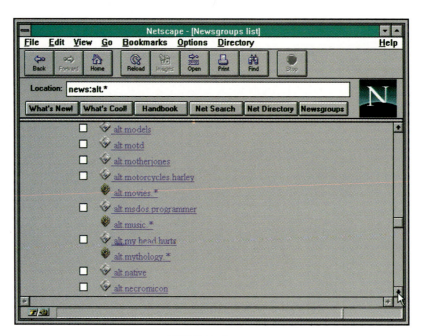

FIGURE HOE2-6

3. Select a news group that interests you.
4. Read the articles posted in the news group.
5. Print one of the articles and turn it in to your instructor.

HANDS-ON EXERCISE 7
Sending Electronic Mail

Purpose: To understand how to send electronic mail messages.

Instructions: Start Netscape and perform the following tasks with a computer.

1. US Senate e-mail addresses can be found at gopher://gopher.senate.gov (Figure HOE2-7). U.S. House of Representatives' email addresses can be found at gopher://gopher.house.gov. Choose one of these two gophers and connect to it.

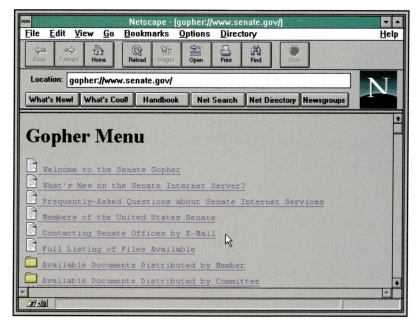

FIGURE HOE2-7

2. Click Contacting Senate/House Offices by E-Mail.
3. Find one of your state's representative's e-mail address. If you cannot find your state in the list, choose a representative with whom you are familiar.
4. Send your representative an electronic mail message concerning a subject that is important to you.
5. Send a copy of the message to your instructor using e-mail.

POPULAR WEB SITES

This appendix contains the URLs for interesting and useful Web sites categorized by topic. Each URL entry contains a brief description of what you can find at the site. At the end of the appendix is a list of public access FTP and gopher sites. You can also obtain additional URLs for popular Web sites by accessing the Shelly Cashman Online Web page at http://www.thomson.com/scstudnt.html.

▶ ART

Largest art gallery on the Web   http://www.mgainc.com/HomePage.html
Links to Louvre, Paris art museum and more   http://venus.mcs.com/~flowers/html.art.html
Photos, images, paintings   http://www.nets.com/site/art/art.html

▶ BUSINESS

Entrepreneur advertising   http://www.moscow.com
Fidelity Investments/Mutual Funds   http://www.fid-inv.com
Small Business Administration   http://www.sbaonline.sba.gov
Networth   http://www.networth.com

▶ ENTERTAINMENT

Fox broadcasting network show pages   http://www.eden.com/users/my-html/fox.html
Trivia quiz   http://altair.herts.ac.uk:8000/html/WebQuiz.html
TV shows from all the networks   http://www.cinenet.net/UTVL/utvl.html

▶ GOVERNMENT

Federal government information source   http://www.fedworld.gov
NASA home page   http://www.gsfc.nasa.gov/NASA_homepage.html
U.S. Geological Survey home page   http://info.er.usgs.gov

▶ INTERNET RELAY CHAT

Chat 1   http://www2.infi.net/talker
Chat 2   http://www.kajen.malmo/se/webchat.html
Chat 3   http://www.irsociety.com/webchat.html

▶ JOBS

Career Fair for College Graduates   http://www.monster.com
Career Mosaic   http://www.service.com/cm/cm1.html
Education Careers   http://chronicle.merit.edu

▶ LAW

Human Rights Web site	http://www.traveller.com/~hrweb/hrweb.html
Legal Information Institute	http://www.law.cornell.edu
U.S. patent database	http://town.hall.org/patent/patent.html

▶ MISCELLANEOUS

Life	http://pathfinder.com/Life/lifehome.html
Planet Earth home page	http://white.nosc.mil/info_modern.html
Rolling Stones Web page	http://www.stones.com
Wired magazine online	http://www.wired.com

▶ MUSEUMS

Chicago Field Museum of Natural History	http://www.bvis.uic.edu/museum
Hands-on science experiments	http://www.exploratorium.edu
Interactive Natural History Museum	http://ucmp1.berkeley.edu

▶ MUSIC

Buy tickets online	http://www.ticketron.com
Contains Web pages for bands	http://www.rock.net
Ticketmaster	http://www.ticketmaster.com
Sample sound files of various bands	http://sunsite.unc.edu/ianc/index.html

▶ SHOPPING

Internet Mall	http://www.kei.com/imall
Internet Shopping Network	http://www.internet.net/directories.html

▶ FTP SITES

Games 1	ftp://ftp.wustl.edu
Games 2	ftp://ftp.nsca.uiuc.edu
Electronic books	ftp://ftp.spies.com
Pictures, sound files	ftp://sunsite.unc.edu
Space pictures	ftp://sseop.jsc.nasa.gov

▶ GOPHER SITES

National Archives	gopher://gopher.loc.gov
Project Gutenburg	gopher://gopher.std.com
Resume database	gopher://garnet.msen.com
Smithsonian Institute Photographs	gopher://gopher.pipeline.com
U.S. census information	gopher://gopher.micro.umn.edu

INSTALLING THE EUDORA MAIL PROGRAM

This appendix details the steps to install the Eudora mail program. To carry out these steps, you must have the eudor144.zip and unzip.exe files on a diskette. See page N73 to retrieve the Eudora and Unzip programs.

Step 1: Insert the diskette with the eudor144.zip and unzip.exe files in drive A.

Step 2: With Program Manager active, select the File menu and choose the Run command.
The Run dialog box displays.

Step 3: Type `command` and press the ENTER key.
A DOS command prompt displays.

Step 4: Type `cd \` and press the ENTER key. Type `mkdir email` and press the ENTER key. Type `cd email` and press the ENTER key.
The DOS command prompt redisplays with email as the active subdirectory.

Step 5: Type `copy a:eudor144.zip` and press the ENTER key. Type `copy a:unzip.exe` and press the ENTER key.
The eudor144.zip file and the unzip.exe file are copied from the diskette in drive A to the email subdirectory.

Step 6: Type `unzip eudor144.zip` and press the ENTER key. Type `exit` and press the ENTER key.
Three files are unzipped and stored in the email subdirectory. The Program Manager window redisplays.

Step 7: With Program Manager active, select the File menu and choose the New command.
The New Program Object dialog box displays.

Step 8: Click Program Group and then choose OK. Type `EMAIL` and choose OK.
A new group window titled EMAIL displays.

Step 9: With Program Manager active, select the File menu and choose the New command. Click Program Item and then choose OK.
The Program Item Properties dialog box displays.

Step 10: In the Description text box, type `Eudora`. Press the TAB key until the insertion point is in the Command Line text box. Type `c:\email\weudora.exe` and choose OK.
A new program-item icon displays in the EMAIL group window.

Step 11: Start Eudora by double-clicking the Eudora program-item icon.
The Eudora window displays.

Step 12: Select the Special menu and choose the Configuration command.
The Configuration dialog box displays.

Step 13: Enter your e-mail address twice, once in the Pop Account text box and once in the Return Address text box. Enter your full name in the Real Name text box.

Step 14: Choose the OK button in the Configuration dialog box.

Step 15: Double-click the Control-menu box in the upper left corner of the Eudora window to close Eudora

You can now double-click the Eudora program-item icon in the EMAIL group window to start Eudora, and follow the instructions on page N108 to read your mail.

INDEX

@ character, e-mail and, N102

Active link indicator, **N7**
  transferring page and, N9
Add Bookmark command, N17
Animation, N3
Articles, news groups and, N90, N92-95
  posting, N87, N96-99
  printing, N95
  saving, N95
Audit trail, **N110**

Back button, **N13**, N14, N79, N81
BACKSPACE key, deleting characters with, N9
Bookmark, N6, **N17**-22
  FTP sites for, N73
  removing, N19-21
  retrieving Web page using, N18-19
Bookmark list
  restoring, N22
  saving, N22
Bookmarks menu
  Add Bookmark command, N17
  Close command, N18
  retrieving Web page using, N18-19
  View Bookmarks command, N17, N19-20, N22
Browsers, **N4**
Browsing the Web, N8-13
  features assisting, N5

Categories, Yahoo directory and, N69
Chat button, N38, N41
Check Mail command, N109
Clear Query Text button, N63
Click here to enter WebChat button, N36
Clipboard, **N26**-32
Close command, Bookmarks menu, N18
Comment text box, N40, N41
Continue button, WebChat and, N36
Conversations, WebChat and, N34-42
Copy command, N29
Copy function, N6
Copying text from Web page, and pasting in
  Notepad, N28-30
Current directory, **N75**

Delete command, e-mail and, N113
Deleting
  bookmarks, N19-21
  characters using BACKSPACE key, N9
  e-mail message, N112-113
  spaces, N30
Directory/directories
  current, N75
  FTP sites, N75-78
  Yahoo, N68-73
Directory buttons, **N6**
Discussion groups
  WebChat and, N34-42
  USENET and, N87
Diskette
  copying FTP site files onto, N79-80
  saving bookmark on, N22
  saving e-mail message to, N110-111
  saving Notepad document to, N31
  saving Web page to, N23
Display area, **N5**
  transferring page and, N9, N10
Documents, **N4**
Domain name, **N7**
Drives drop-down list box, N22, N24, N31, N80

Editing bookmarks, N19-21
Edit menu

Copy command, N29
  Paste command, N30
Electronic mail, *see* e-mail
Electronic mail address, **N102**
e-mail, N6, **N102**-113
  adding personality to, N107
  audit trail, N110
  deleting message, N112-113
  preparing to use, N102-104
  printing message, N111-112
  reading using Eudora, N102, N107-113
  saving message to disk, N110-111
  sending, N104-107
Enter Password dialog box, N109
Error correction, N9
Eudora, N73-82, **N107**-113
  exiting, N113
  search for, N75
  starting, N107-108
Eudora group window, N108
Exiting
  Eudora, N113
  Netscape, N46
Export Bookmarks button, N22
Export Bookmarks dialog box, N22

File(s)
  mail box, N104
  Notepad, N26-32
  retrieving using gopher, N82-86
  retrieving with FTP, N73-82
  transferring with FTP, N73
  unzipping, N81-82
  zipped, N78
File management, N6
File menu, N6
  Check Mail command, N109
  Mail document command, N105
  Print command, N33, N111-112
  Save as command, N23, N31, N111
File specification, of Web page, N7
File Transfer Protocol, *see* FTP
Forms, **N34**, N37
  InfoSeek input, N58-61
Forward button, **N13**, N15
FTP (File Transfer Protocol), **N73**
  retrieving files with, N73-82
FTP archives, **N73**
FTP directories, public access, N75-81
FTP sites, N73
  Eudora and, N107

Go menu
  displaying Web page using history list and, N16
  Internet Directory page, N72
  Internet Search page, N62
Gopher, **N82**-86
Gopher Menu page, N83
Gopher menus, navigating, N84-86
Graphics, N3

Handbook command, N43
Handbook directory button, N45
Handle, **N37**
  choosing, N39
Help, N6, N43-45
Help menu, N45
  Handbook command, N43
History functions, N6
History list, **N13**-17
  returning to Internet Search page using, N62
Home button, N18
Home page, **N4**
  Welcome To Netscape, N5, N8, N35

HTTP (HyperText Transport Protocol), **N7**
Hypermedia, **N3**
  documents, N4
Hypermedia page management, N6
Hypertext link, **N3**
  FTP sites and, N76-77
  gopher and, N84-85
  InfoSeek and, N60-61
  picture set up as, N10
  underlined blue words, N5
  WebCrawler and, N63-67
  Yahoo Directory and, N68-73
HyperText Transport Protocol, *see* HTTP

Icons, FTP site and, N75
Image, saving, N25
Indexes
  FTP sites, N79
  online Help and, N43, N45
  WebCrawler and, N63
InfoSeek, **N58**-61, N73
InfoSeek Corporation, N58
InfoSeek input form, N58-61
In mail box, N109-110
Insertion point, **N13**
Internet, **N2**
  browsers, N4
  conversing over, N34-42
  hypertext link and, N3
  multimedia capability, N3
  World Wide Web and, N3-4
Internet address, N7
Internet Directory page, N68, N72
Internet Roundtable society, N34-42
Internet Search page, N58
  displaying, N63
  returning to, N62-63

JPEG, encoding pictures and, **N15**

Keywords
  using InfoSeek to search for, N59-61
  WebCrawler and, N64-65
Keywords text box, N59

Link, *see* Hypertext link

Mail, *see* e-mail
Mail and News dialog box, N104
Mail and News preference, N103
Mail box, **N104**
Mail Document command, N105
Mail server, **N108**-110
Mail to:box, N106
Menu bar, **N6**
Message(s), e-mail and, N102-113
Message menu, Delete command, N113
Message text box, N106
Microsoft Accessories group window, N26
Mosaic, N4
Mouse pointer, hypertext link and, N5

Net Directory button, N8, N68
Net in Arcadia, N8-11
Netscape
  accessing USENET with, N87-90
  e-mail and, N102-113
  exiting, N46
  gopher and, N82-86
  home page, N5, N18
  introduction to, N2-46
  news groups and, N87-102
  printing Web page in, N32-33
  retrieving files with FTP, N73-82

N127